The Best C⋯⋯g Guide

The Best Counselling Guide

Where to go, what to expect, and how to
get the help you need

Susan Quilliam
and
Ian Grove-Stephensen

Thorsons
An Imprint of HarperCollins*Publishers*

Thorsons
A Division of HarperCollins*Publishers*
77-85 Fulham Palace Road,
Hammersmith, London W6 8JB

First published by Thorsons 1990
as *The Counselling Handbook*
This revised edition published 1991
10 9 8 7 6 5 4 3 2 1

© Transformation Management 1990, 1991

Susan Quilliam and Ian Grove-Stephensen assert the moral right to
be identified as the authors of this work

A catalogue record for this book
is available from the British Library

ISBN 0 7225 2612 1

Printed in Great Britain by
Biddles of Guildford, Kent
Typesetting by MJL Limited,
Hitchin, Hertfordshire

Contents

Acknowledgements

We should like to thank everyone who, over the course of our lives, and in particular during our careers as clients, counsellors and teachers of counselling, have helped us to prepare for writing this book. The ideas in it are peculiarly our own, but they have been developed by the stimulation, the inspiration and sometimes the wonderful frustration of being with these people! Thank you.

In particular, in the preparation of this book, we should like to thank the following, and many other people who chose not to be named:

Carlye Honig; Derek Blows, Director of the Westminster Pastoral Foundation; Evelyn; Gill Bannister, full member of IPC (WPF); James Nichol MA, Dip NLP, AIPTI; Janet Friedman; Janet Rimmer; Jo Spence; John Fielder MBIM, MITD, MISM, MECI; Martin Leith; Mike Owen; Sue Mack, counsellor; Rosamund; Rose Danielle DHP; Students at the Westminster Pastoral Foundation; Tamara Batt; Charles Goodson, CQSW, Dip Adl Couns., BAC (Accd) Couns., FIIP.

A special thank you to Tony Renshaw for suggesting the original title for the book.

Foreword

by Norman Keir
Chairman of the Samaritans

The benefits of sharing one's uncertainties with a trusted confidant have long been known. Moses, overwhelmed by his judicial responsibilities, had a useful talk with his father-in-law, who listened attentively and then offered excellent advice (delegate!) The Greeks, including that most decisive of them, Alexander the Great, consulted the Oracles. The response they received was often ambiguous, even misleading. But presumably they found it helpful to have what, more than two millennia later, T S Eliot called 'the luxury of an intimate disclosure to a stranger'. For those in dire trouble, of course, it may have been much more than a mere luxury, in the same way that the sharing of suicidal feelings with a Samaritan can be a matter of life or death.

In these ancient times, there were probably few agencies which offered a listening ear. Now we are faced with a bewildering choice, and words like 'counselling' and 'therapy' have a wide spectrum of connotations. Some counsellors give advice, thereby fulfilling what the dictionary definition of their occupation suggests is their role; most do not, believing that to be directive is to be unhelpful. The potential client is understandably perplexed. So Susan Quilliam and Ian Grove-Stephensen's comprehensive, user-friendly, practical manual is most welcome.

This book is about counsellors — who are professional friends — and the therapeutic relationship which they offer. The language of friendship, Thoreau said, is not words but meanings. It is through the sharing of words with a professional friend that clients may find the meanings they seek.

Norman Keir

Introduction

This is *The Counselling Handbook*. The title raises two questions. What exactly is counselling — and why do we need a handbook about it?

By counselling, we mean an extension of the kind of support which in the past was naturally provided by our social structure. In previous ages, the extended family and the village support system often provided a helping hand and a listening ear when we had a problem, suffered a crisis, or questioned our lives and our identities. Now it's not quite so easy. The extended family has been replaced by the fractured community, the village support system by the state welfare apparatus. More and more, we are turning to outside help — to counselling — to get our needs met.

Who provides this outside help? Counsellors are people who combine the best qualities of the friendship that our society offered in the past with the best aspects of the professionalism it provides now. Counsellors will, like friends, listen, support, challenge — and stand by while you work things out for yourself. They will also, as professionals, make a clear contract with you — their time, skill and expertise for your time and often your money. They add to this professional contract their emotion and their commitment; the best of them give you the resources to do the same.

Nowadays, more and more, we see counsellors and counselling as a beneficial part of our lives, our friends lives, our children's lives. We watch television programmes with a counselling element, not only for interest, but also because they are relevant to our own situations. Whether we receive counselling to maximize the effect of medical treatment, ring the Samaritans when we are desperate, or use long-term psychotherapy to increase our everyday enjoyment of life, we are part of an increasing body of users, people who need and benefit from counselling services. We have become consumers, and as such, we are beginning to become aware of what we as consumers need and how to get it.

Why?

A while ago — as consumers ourselves as well as providers — we recognized a curious phenomenon. Counsellors themselves often get years of training to enable them to 'do the best for' their clients. But as clients, however, we get no help in getting the best for ourselves.

What was needed, we thought, was a consumers' handbook. Not a detailed listing of every counsellor available — they come and go, change style or fee, shift their ideas of what they are doing. Not even a recommendation of what works and what doesn't, for unlike washing-machines, the usefulness and relevance of counselling will vary from client to client. Rather, what was needed was a handbook to enable consumers to find out what they want from counsellors and counselling, and then get it.

This is that book. It is for you if you have never received counselling before, because it is very straightforward and untheoretical in its approach. It is also for you if you are receiving counselling and want to know how you can become more actively involved. It is certainly a book for you if you are a counsellor, or hope to become one, as it will help you establish a basic framework around what you are doing.

What the book will do is this:

- It will help you to work out what you want from counselling.
- It will show you how to find the counsellor or organization most likely to help you achieve what you want.
- It will give you enough basic information to help you to develop a sense of whether you are getting a truly professional service.

- It will tell you what to do if you are not achieving the results you want.

This is a reference and resource book which you can dip into rather than a book to read from cover to cover. The book is diagnostic in that it presumes you need to identify an issue and then deal with it. The layout, in short sections, with check-lists and cross-references, is intended to help you to do this. You can use the chapter headings to identify and look at the sections that are most relevant to your issue.

What won't this book do? It won't give you the complete theoretical background to the counselling you may receive, in the same way as the *WHICH?* report doesn't tell you all about the mechanics of tumble driers. It won't give any kind of exhaustive listing of individuals or organizations; there are hundreds of counselling organizations already in existence and more spring up each week, while the number of individual counsellors available runs into tens of thousands. And it won't, indeed can't, tell you exactly what you and your particular counsellor will do in each particular session — that is up to you.

About us

Between us, we have been involved in counselling for a total of sixteen years. Over this span of time, we have developed both personally and professionally in ways that we would not have dreamed possible when we first started on the counselling adventure. Indeed, they would not have *been* possible had it not been for the time, money and commitment that we both put into counselling, being counselled individually and being members of groups. Knowing the incredible benefits, and having also experienced at first-hand the pitfalls of counselling, we have become committed to setting up exactly the right sort of context in which it can operate.

We have also both experienced and practised a variety of counselling techniques and theories. Two in particular have both delighted and influenced us. *Co-Counselling*, which allows you to train as both client and counsellor, has a wonderfully equal and flexible approach to the art of counselling. And *Neuro-Linguistic Programming* has allowed us to realize the extent to which new ideas can speed up the previously slow and, for many, painful process of change.

As counsellors then, we came to write this book with a number of personal experiences. As authors, we added to these by interviewing a number of clients, counsellors and trainee counsellors in a variety of schools and approaches, especially in those of which we had little prior experience. Some of these interviews are reproduced verbatim in Chapters 12 and 13, but many more underlie the body of the book, and many of the opinions you will find here are those of our interviewees.

However, we also include our opinions and, in some places, our frustrations. We believe that our contribution to this book is to offer a model of preference and choice — if we are clear about our preferences, this will allow you, the reader, to be equally clear about yours. Our ultimate aim is that this book will encourage you to go for what you want, whatever that is, even if (particularly if) we don't happen to agree with it!

A final thought...

If there is just one thing we would like you to learn from this book, it is this. You deserve to get what you want, both in counselling and out of it. You deserve to have the best counselling you can get.

Section 1

The process

Chapter 1

Do you need counselling?

Before you begin, the first question to ask yourself is, obviously; Do I need a counsellor? Do I, in fact, need or want counselling at all? It is a basic and often crucial question.

For Jill, whose mother spent most of her adulthood in and out of analysis, and who used it as an excuse to withdraw into herself and neglect her daughter, the idea of counselling may be a negative one. For Simon, whose wife recovered from her miscarriage largely due to the sympathetic support of a trained counsellor, the idea is positive. For many people, particularly those who have never been in counselling, or have only heard about it second-hand, it may seem that anyone who undergoes counselling is 'odd', 'a bit funny' or 'not coping'. Negative judgements are often made on anyone who sometimes finds life too much for them and actually has the cheek to go out and do something about it.

We suspect that out of every ten people who walk into a doctor's surgery, nine are there because they need psychological rather than physical support. To turn to others for help to cope with a crisis, deal with stress or simply think things through is a normal human response.

How to use this chapter

Our aim in this chapter is to help you decide whether counselling is appropriate for you. We do this in a number of ways.

- First, we offer you some ideas of the nature of counselling which are common among people who are clients and counsellors themselves.

- We then look at what counselling offers, inviting you to consider whether these things are what you need.

- Next, we point out some things that counselling *doesn't* do.

- We go on to examine whether in fact, you would be better finding help from your existing support system and offer an exploration to enable you to discover this.

- Finally, again using an exploration, we look at any final blocks you may have against finding counselling help.

Dip into this chapter to find out more about what counselling is, and to decide, particularly by doing the explorations, whether it is relevant for you.

What is counselling?

We gathered, over the course of our interviews, some agreement on what counselling involves, together with a vast variation of different definitions of what it is.

The agreement seemed to be about the practicalities. Our interviewees seemed to have a common image of 'counselling' as something that takes place between 'counsellor' and 'client', whether in pairs, or small or large groups. It can be via telephone contact or face-to-face. It can be two people meeting privately or working in groups or as part of a whole, huge organization. It can be paid or unpaid.

The variations we found were to do with people's definitions of what counselling was about. Different counsellors gave different examples — some clients saw the whole thing as different again. These are some of the most useful definitions we were given.

Counselling is *contractual*

This aspect of counselling turns what could be just a friendly chat into a professional situation. In a counselling relationship, you formally agree with your counsellor that you are working together to help you achieve the outcomes you have discussed.

This spoken (or even written) contract may include: practical details about time (the length of session, the number of sessions); money (price per session, a fixed fee) and commitment (not missing sessions). But you will also have another contract with your counsellor which involves agreements about the way you will work together and what you can expect from each other. This contract may not be overt, but it will be there. The British Association of Counselling, in their definition, says that the counsellor 'offers and agrees explicitly to give time, attention and respect. . .' We like that definition and hope that this book helps to support it.

Counselling is *caring*

Many people feel that a counsellor is someone who is on their side, who offers caring support of all kinds — practical, emotional, psychological — in a way that a close relative or friend often can't. Liz was typical of the people we talked to when she commented that 'The issues I need counselling on are ones I don't choose to share with people close to me. I don't want to burden them — and I don't want them to know.' Usually, clients felt that their counsellors care for them, though, for both clients and counsellors, there is disagreement about the most appropriate ways of caring. Marsailli said that 'I thought my counsellor didn't care because often he didn't touch me. I only realize now that he knew what he was doing — he was caring by giving me an experience of being independent.'

Counselling is *challenging*

Some people say that an essential part of counselling for them is challenge. A counsellor's role is often to question what a client does, and to make the client think twice about it. Tony said that the most helpful thing his counsellor had done for him was to challenge his decision to stay in a failing marriage and help him to realize that this wasn't what he really wanted to do. 'In the beginning, I just couldn't listen to what she was saying — it took a while for me even to consider it.' For both client and counsellor, it may be hard to hear a challenge rather than an agreement, but often it is vital.

Counselling is *explorative*

When counsellor and client start working together, it may be clear what the issue is that they are dealing with; Sally, who turned to a specialist counselling agency for help with her drinking, had a specific problem to tackle. Often, however, people turn to counselling because of an unspecific need, a feeling of dissatisfaction or a general belief that they are not doing as well as they should in the world. Whatever seems to be the reason for beginning counselling, it will take some exploration to find out what the real issue is. Sally discovered that her drinking was not the real problem, but a symptom of her underlying lack of self-confidence. Good counsellors will always help their clients through a voyage of exploration and discovery.

Counselling *goes from conscious to unconscious*

The counsellors we talked to were eager to stress that counselling is not only about what we are aware of. It is also about beginning to realize things we are not aware of. 'I help people to bring their unconscious feelings, thoughts and needs into consciousness, where we can deal with them,' said Charles, an Adlerian[1] counsellor. This doesn't mean that all counsellors will be delving into your innermost secrets — a good counsellor allows you to go at your own pace and in your own way. It is useful, though, to have someone who can spot when you are not aware of things about your own situation, and help you realize what these are.

Counselling is *confidential*

The usual contract in counselling is that what you say to your counsellor is for his or her ears alone. Unlike confidentiality contracts in other professions, such as with doctors or priests, this can sometimes be renegotiated; nevertheless, you should expect such a contract from your counsellor, and be prepared to check that it is being kept to. Should your counsellor tell you confidential information — for example, what he has written on your case notes? This is a bone of contention; some say it is not useful for you to know 'an expert's view'; others, like John, a career counsellor say that, 'you have to be prepared to own up to whatever you write.'

[1] See Chapter 15.

Counselling is *conclusive*

If it is to be seen as successful, all counselling needs to provide a resolution or conclusion to whatever brought you to counselling in the first place. Many of the people we talked to spoke of their counselling experiences as providing 'an answer', even though this may have been by raising more questions. Many of them said that, through counselling, they were able to come to terms with their issues in a positive way, whether this is resolving an unhappy relationship or saying goodbye to a deceased partner. By 'conclusive', we also want to point out that counselling does not have to go on forever — it needs to have a conclusion. The British Association for Counselling makes a nice point in its definition when it says that 'a person... (is) *temporarily* in the role of client.' [our italics]

Counselling is *empowering*

One myth about counselling is that counsellors will tell you what to do with your life. In fact, many of the counsellors we spoke to stressed the exact opposite. '*You* are the person who knows about your life. *You* are the expert on your life; a good counsellor will use *your* expertise,' said Evelyn, who specializes in telephone counselling. Of course, some forms of counselling do involve giving advice — but good counsellors still make sure that you don't feel deskilled or patronized. In addition, good counsellors give you the right to decide what is right for you, your 'ultimate right to self-determination.' The classic example of this is the Samaritans organization, whose principles state that 'a caller does not lose the freedom to make his own decisions, including the decision to take his own life'. (Principles).

Counselling is *psychotherapy?*

Many people are confused about the difference between counselling and psychotherapy. We spoke to counsellors who said they regarded themselves as therapists; we spoke to therapists who said they were counsellors; we spoke to both counselling and therapy organizations who defended their right to their particular label, and we noticed that the BAC mentioned 'psychotherapeutic' as one of its categories of counselling.

In the course of our research we collected a catalogue of completely contradictory definitions of the two words. However, when we asked a number of professionals why *they* chose the label they did, off the record, quite a number admitted that it was a marketing strategy: 'counselling' sounds safer, 'therapy' sounds more daring.

For the purposes of this book, we have excluded people who *only* give advice (like financial counsellors) and people in the helping professions who include some counselling but in a wider context (like nurses, the clergy and social workers). Otherwise we have tried to include everyone whose main *activities* fall roughly into the guidelines outlined in this section and have ignored the *label* under which they market their services. We use the word 'counsellors' to avoid chopping and changing between all the possibilities, and hope that we don't offend too many people.

What does counselling offer?

Various situations could prompt you to look for counselling. You, are, perhaps, feeling generally low, unsatisfied, unfulfilled. It could be that you are getting messages from the outside world that all is not right — an illness, a complaint from your boss, a failing relationship. You could be suffering some specific problem such as drug or alcohol abuse or a sexual issue. Or, you may simply be looking to make a good life better.

What can counselling offer you in these situations? It seems that it can help in a number of ways. For the moment, we've simplified them to four general *functions*. Most counsellors offer a blend of each of these functions, and, of course, your needs will be a combination of all of them.

Information

James was diagnosed HIV-positive. Realizing that he needed outside help, he and his wife Jenny went to their local AIDS counselling service. 'I wanted to know,' said James, 'what the facts were, what could I do, what couldn't I do, what the chances were.' James and Jenny didn't only need someone to talk to; they needed information. Many counselling organizations offer information as part of their service. If you are seeking career counselling, for example, your counsellor will certainly offer you support, and insight into your career needs, but when you have this, he will then also be able to give you the information to proceed. Some rape or drugs counselling services also offer legal advice and information alongside their support services.

In general, however, if what you need is *primarily* information, you are *probably* not in need of counselling. So, for example, if the help you need at the moment is to know where to complain about your rates bill, what you need most is not a counsellor but the number of an advice service.

Support

Counselling will almost certainly offer you support. For many people, this is the first, the key, sometimes the only thing they need from a counselling relationship. 'Once I trusted her,' said Marie, who sought counselling after the break up of a relationship, 'I basically spent most of the time crying and letting her tell me I was okay.'

Remember, however, that, as we mentioned earlier, the counsellors and counselling organizations we spoke to, who all agreed that support was a large part of their role, varied in their definition of that word; we spoke to one drug dependency counsellor who told us that on occasions, 'Telling my clients the brutal truth is the best way I can support them.' So be clear about what 'support' means to you.

Insight

Many of the people we talked to expressed a deep-seated aim to 'understand what is happening' through their counselling. Rod's divorce had plunged him into a depression he did not understand. 'We wanted to split up, it was all very civilized, so why the kickback?' Through counselling, he traced his bad feelings back to an experience of abandonment when he was a child and his father had been away in the forces. By linking up the two crises and understanding how they related to each other, Rod began to feel he had some choice about his depression.

On the other hand, we did speak to clients who felt that they did not need to understand. 'What is there to understand about his dying?' said one woman. 'It happened, that's all'. Also, some forms of counselling work on the basis that insight is not always necessary for a successful outcome — if a client changes their behaviour or feelings to more positive ones than before, that is enough.

Change

Whether they state this clearly or not, we believe that the goal of all counsellors, counselling forms and counselling theories is to offer the client change towards 'greater well-being' (BAC). If you are not happy, you will want to change in order to be happier. If you are less effective than you would like, you will want to change in order to be more effective.

Where counselling methods differ from each other is the way in which they see change happening. Some schools of thought, like NLP[2], point out that it takes a fifth of a second to change your mind, and so a change of heart should take no longer and be no more difficult. On the other hand, I was told that in order to achieve a real breakthrough,

---

Jane, a teacher in her mid-twenties, thought she was going to a counsellor only for support after her husband died of cancer. She spent the first weeks simply crying and her counsellor spent the first weeks simply listening. When Jane was ready, her counsellor suggested that she look more deeply at her relationship with her husband, and her relationship with her parents, particularly her father. Jane began to realize that a great deal of her distress stemmed back to her own early childhood experiences and her guilt around her father's continuing illnesses. On one particular day, after a bout of weeping, she was able to say, 'I am not responsible for Tom's [her husband's] death and I am not responsible for Dad's death. They are not my fault.' After saying this, she suddenly started to laugh, almost hysterically, for many minutes, and then became calm. With these insights came a change in the way she saw the future. Instead of planning a life devoted to 'making amends' for Tom's death, she began to be able to choose to enjoy herself and maybe even to consider marrying again.

---

[2] See Chapter 15.

I should commit for between ten to fifteen years' commented Helen, working with a psychoanalyst.

In addition, remember that a change in your well-being will always effect a change in your whole life-style. If you decide that you want change, you need to be prepared, as we point out in Chapter 7, to accept this.

What counselling *won't* do

In an overwhelming majority of cases, counselling *will* help you if you feel bad. In an equally overwhelming majority of cases, though, counselling *will not* make you feel universally wonderful. In order to give a balanced viewpoint on counselling, therefore, we'd like to mention some of the things counselling *can't* do. After reading it, you may decide that counselling is not for you after all. If you do go ahead, it will be in an informed way.

- *Counselling can change you, but it won't change the world.* Counselling of any kind will never make other people any different, add value to your house, remove the noisy neighbours. It can alter the way you handle these things, and whether they continue to bother you, but it can't change the things themselves.

- *Counselling won't solve all your problems.* If you go to a counsellor with a specific issue — for example, eating problems — it is likely that solving this issue will have a knock-on effect on your life, and other problems may well resolve themselves. But counselling won't magic away every bad feeling you have, or necessarily deal with issues you haven't even mentioned to the counsellor.

- *Counselling isn't a substitute for love or friendship.* Although some counselling agencies offer a befriending service, the aim of counselling is to get you to a point where you can make and keep friends and loved ones of your own.

- *Counselling can't make any of the benefits happen if you don't want them to.* This works two ways. Firstly, it is not possible for a counsellor to change or affect you 'by magic' in ways you don't want. You are not under their spell, and they are not magicians. Of course it also means that in order to get the benefits, you too have to take responsibility. It takes two to tango.

What else would do instead of counselling?

You may already have around you a support system composed of friends, family and colleagues. Would they, in fact, serve you better than counsellors would?

The way to decide this is to look at what each has to offer. Counsellors have a very particular role to play, offering expertise, objectivity and accessibility where friends, relatives, priests and lovers may not. But people within your existing social circle can offer more of other things such as physical comfort, a supportive belief system, or a lifetime's knowledge of you.

Mark tried to cope on his own when he was made redundant. He and his family were very hard-hit, both financially and emotionally, but it was a point of pride to Mark that they didn't ask for outside help. However, his depression and bad temper put such a strain on his marriage that, at last, his wife said that unless he sought professional counselling, she would leave with the children. With his hand forced like this, Mark did seek professional help. One of the first things his counsellor was able to help him realize was that asking for outside help was a sign of maturity and being able to cope. Given the right support, Mark was able to work through his emotional reactions, and although he has still not got a job, he is now more able to support his wife in her work.

Here is an exploration to help you decide which to choose. The grid lists possible people in your life — fill in the names of the relevant people in the spaces. Each of them could fulfil one or more of the generic functions of information, support, insight and change. Write down just what benefits you will get from each of them — and what their limitations are.

	Information	Support	Insight	Change	Limitations
Best friend					
Friend					
Spouse					
Lover					
Children					
Social worker					
Religious leader					
Doctor					
Relatives					

When you have completed the grid, take time to think it
through and perhaps talk it through with a friend. Ask yourself whether you are using your current available support
system to the full and whether you would be better served
by going outside it. What are you not asking from those
around you that you could ask of them? What missing elements are there that you could easily fulfil? What possible
resources are open to you that you're not using? What blocks
are there to your using your existing support system to meet
your needs? If, finally, you are sure that it is either impossible or simply undesirable to have your needs met by your
current support system, then you have a clear motivation
to go into counselling.

Final blocks?

You may still have some misgivings. Despite the fact that you feel good about the idea of counselling, that you realize it may meet your needs, and that you have decided to seek professional counsellors rather than call on your already existing social network, you may still be hesitant.

Here is an exercise to help you finally decide. Take time on your own to read through the following suggestions for day dreams. You may want to allow yourself thinking space in a relaxed place or somewhere quiet. You may want to make notes on your responses to each of the next three paragraphs.

● Consider your worst fantasy about counselling. Are you afraid that the counsellor will laugh, get angry, stay silent, ignore you? Are you afraid that your problem is too big, too small, too shocking? Perhaps you will spend lots of money and get no return — or waste lots of time and realize it too late to do anything about your situation.

● What would be the absolute best that could happen? If all your most positive ideas of counselling were fulfilled, what would be the outcome? This may help you contact a feeling of optimism — after all, it might happen.

● Thirdly, taking your fears and fantasies into account, ask yourself what the minimum commitment would be that you could make to counselling. A test session? A phone call? To ask a friend for a counsellor's address?

When you have thought through all these questions, either you will know for sure that counselling is not for you, or you will have decided on a minimum step you can take. We suggest, if you can, that you at least take this first step. You don't have to go any further, but you will at least find out how you feel after having taken it. If you still feel unhappy about it, perhaps counselling isn't right for you at present. If you begin to feel hopeful, maybe taking one step towards counselling has shown you that it is right to take another step towards it.

Chapter 2

What counselling do you need?

There are many different kinds of counselling, and many different kinds of counsellor. You will get the best possible service if you are clear about exactly what kind you want. This chapter helps you to identify exactly what it is that you want from a counsellor and from counselling. It looks at the following issues, which we found to be ones mentioned most often by the interviewees we spoke to:

- *What sort of counselling do you need* — in terms of function, starting points, school, style, form?

- *What kind of counsellor do you need* — in terms of gender, culture, age, preferences?

- *What have you to offer in return for the counselling you want* — in terms of money, time, other commitments?

Use this chapter to identify your needs and preferences. At the end of this chapter is an exploration grid. As you read through the chapter and learn more about your particular needs, you may want to fill the grid in. When you have finished, you will have a complete set of notes on your situation. We suggest that you repeat the exercise in the future whenever you change counsellors, and even during your work with one particular counsellor. This will help you both to keep track of how your needs are changing, and to check that your needs are being met.

What kind of counselling do you need?

There are a number of things to think of when you are deciding what kind of counselling you want. Many of them, such as the particular kind of session you get most from, you can only decide *after* you have started counselling with one particular counsellor. We have identified several factors for you to consider in advance, or to rethink once you have begun counselling.

Function

Many of our interviewees mentioned that they were looking for particular needs to be met in their counselling. It seems that whatever your starting point for counselling, this will, as we mentioned in chapter 1, be underpinned by a set of basic needs and wants which we called *general functions*. We divide them into four basic types — the need for *information*, the need for *support*, the need for *insight* and the need for *change*.

You will probably want more than one of these — and counsellors or counselling organizations nearly always provide more than one. Counselling usually includes all four in different combinations. You may want to refresh your memory by reading through our explanations of each function on pages 22-24. Then, ask yourself:

What do I really need in my current situation?

Your answers will probably fall into one of the following groups:

● 'I need to be told how to. . .'
   'I need facts. . .'
   'I need names and addresses. . .'
   'I need the answers to these questions. . .'

If your answers are of this kind, then you will need counselling that includes *information*.

● 'I just want to be allowed to cry (get angry, feel afraid...)'
'I need someone to listen to me.'
'I want to feel I'm OK.'
'I need someone to help me through...'

This kind of answer indicates that you need counselling that includes *support*.

● 'I want to understand...'
'I need to explore...'
'I want to feel differently about...'
'I want to clear up the confusion about...'

This kind of answer would show that you are looking for some sort of *insight* into your situation.

● 'I want to act differently when...'
'I'm not doing as well as I want to in...'
'I need to change...'
'I want to improve my...'

Answers like this would indicate that you are seeking counselling that aims towards *change*.

Starting points

We found that most people we talked to identified one of two main triggers for entering counselling.

● One starting point for many people entering counselling is a specific *issue* they are concerned about. This is usually a shock or crisis which triggers a variety of emotions; a specific medical problem such as drinking or eating disorders; a turning point or time of change in their life such as retirement or job change; a long-term issue such as marital difficulty or the strain of being in some way handicapped. Most clients going to a counsellor for the first time come into this category.

In all these situations, people are usually drawn towards a counsellor or an organization that has a particular expertise in what they see their problem to be. The range of appropriate counsellors is narrowed down immediately, but, at the same time, it becomes easier to make a choice. The majority of people with, for example, drink problems, go to a specialist agency such as Alcoholics Anonymous.[1] Or 'I didn't need to think about where to go — as soon as I heard, I just picked up the phone and dialled my local cancer support group,' said one woman.

We have devoted Chapter 4 of this book to giving you more guidance on what issue-based counselling is available, and you may want to look there now and note down the information you gain from it in the check-list at the end of this chapter.

● Other people we spoke to had no particular issue to trigger their counselling needs. They feel drawn to it because of a *generalized* feeling of need for counselling — or, occasionally, a generalized feeling of attraction to counselling. For Marion, it was a feeling of being unfulfilled. She found herself becoming less and less effective in her job, and more anxious and tired when she was away from it. 'There were no particular symptoms. I knew something was wrong, but I wasn't ill, I wasn't drinking, I just felt there was no point.' For Geoff, on the other hand, it was a desire to know more about himself. 'I felt as if I was delving into a treasure chest, and I wanted to find out what was in there.'

If your concerns are more widespread, if your need for support does not centre around a specific problem or symptom, you may find it both easier and more rewarding to contact a counsellor or agency that deals with more general issues. At the same time, you may find that because your feelings are generalized, it is difficult to get the help you want. The caring professions, particularly if they are tied into the state system, often find it easier to cope with clearly-defined 'problems' than with a generalized feeling of discontent. In the absence of an identifiable issue, you may not even be sure yourself just what it is that you need. 'I was just looking for someone good,' said Martin.

---

[1] Strictly speaking, AA is a peer support organization, not a counselling agency.

Tessa wanted a counsellor who would allow her to let out all the emotion she felt about being abused as a child. Her first search led her to a counsellor whose prime aim was to help her feel better about what had happened. To this end, they worked together over a number of weeks on attempting to change the memories or see them differently, using a variety of techniques based on cognitive therapy. In the end, Tessa changed her counsellor, realizing that although he was 'good', he wasn't what she needed. She went to a more cathartically-based counsellor who allowed her to work out her grief and anger physically in a safe environment. She feels that now she could return to a more 'rational' counselling approach and benefit from it, but that at that time it was wrong for her.

Schools of counselling

Counsellors, like dolphins, are organized into schools. These schools each hold a set of beliefs or use approaches to human development which they consider to be more valid than any of the others.

Very few clients new to counselling chose their counsellor because of the counselling school he or she belonged to. Most people who come into counselling for the first time 'take what you're given' as one woman said. One counsellor commented that he believed the theoretical distinctions between the various counselling schools were of interest only to counsellors, not to clients!

As you get more experience of counselling, it can help to know what background or training a particular person has. It can tell you a lot if you know that one believes in 'brief' therapy while another is into 'non-directive' intervention. However, two counsellors with identical training may approach a client very differently, while another two counsellors who have very different labels may work in the same way. 'I've worked with analysts who let me cry and humanistic counsellors who never say a word!' was one comment.

We give, in Chapter 15, basic explanations of the main schools of counselling, and you can use these to guide and inform your choice. But, for most people, it is far more important to have a general idea of what you want in a session, and not to get too involved in trying to define any type of counselling or counsellor — you will almost certainly run into trouble. However, you may still want to note down on the exploration sheet at the end of this chapter any preferences you may have for one school of counselling over another.

Styles of counselling

Far more important than knowing your potential counsellor's training is to be aware of what you actually want to do in the course of a session. Obviously it is impossible to know precisely what someone will do in a session before working with them, but you can develop a general idea of what you hope to do. You can know, for example, as Tammy did, that, 'There was no way I was going to let anyone push me into bashing cushions.'

We devote Chapter 5 to listing the various activities that may take place in a session, and this will be helpful to you in deciding the sort of counselling you want. At this stage it is worthwhile browsing through that chapter, noting down any elements that positively alarm you and any that really attract you. Bear in mind that all counselling activities are optional — no good counsellor will push you into doing anything you really object to. Use this range of possible activities as a basic guideline to the sort of counselling you would like to have.

Form

One of the main factors in your choice of counsellor is what form your counselling will take.

How many people?
Counselling can be done on a one-to-one basis, as part of a couple, or in a larger group. Individual counselling will guarantee you more attention from your counsellor, and the chance to work on whatever is important to you during each session. It is also usually more expensive, and, certainly in the NHS where resources are thinly spread, may not be an option. If you are having marriage guidance, then counselling in couples is often the most obvious option, although you can choose to work alone if that is what you would prefer.

Many people find that the group situation has a lot to offer: 'I moved from one-to-one group work,' said Julian, 'and found it the best move I made. The fact of having others there who had the same problems that I did helped me not to feel guilty.' Group counselling is also often cheaper than one-to-one counselling, hour-for-hour.

In Co-Counselling[2], you learn how to be both client and counsellor, and often act as both in one-to-one and group settings. This has the advantage of allowing you to see problems from many different perspectives.

Residential or not?
Another issue about the form your counselling may take will be whether to opt for residential or non-residential counselling. Counselling normally takes place in regular visits to the counsellor's home or clinic. However, with some counselling, particularly on issues which involve some form of dependency, a residential course is advisable. It provides a break from your usual surroundings and friends and it plunges you into a whole new way of thinking and behaving. Justin, a recovering alcoholic said 'A residential course was just what I needed; I was far too subject to temptation at home, and the month I spent away gave me the break from my usual lifestyle.' Remember, though, that residential work is often only available on the state system if you are homeless or in a very severe crisis.

What kind of counsellor do you need?

Even if you are going to a counsellor through the NHS system, where little choice is available, it is often possible to choose the counsellor you prefer to work with. Before deciding what you want, however, a word of warning about the whole issue of preference.

Expectations can be a problem
Typically, strongly painful or enjoyable past interactions with

[2] See pages 138, 211-2 and 233.

people make us imagine that others who resemble these people (in, for example, age, gender, cultural outlook), will react in the same way. We sometimes see people as blank screens on to which we 'transfer' our expectations, which may not be relevant to the real person at all.

So, even if your knowledge of counselling comes only through the media or from what people have told you, you may be wary of certain kinds of counsellor. 'I don't want someone who just nods all the time,' said one prospective client; 'I need someone who isn't going to try to make me cry.' said another. Good counsellors neither nod all the time nor have a vested interest in making you cry — the point of these quotations rather is that we all have our expectations and preoccupations, and need to take notice of them if our needs are to be fully met.

Choosing a counsellor because of a particular quality they may have — their age, for example — may be counter-productive, because you are actually judging them on criteria which have nothing to do with the person they really are. 'As soon as I saw Gillian, I knew I could never work with her, because she looked exactly like my sister, and brought up all sorts of thoughts and emotions in me,' said Jim, who later learned that Gillian was, in fact, a very supportive counsellor.

However, the fact is that, try as we might not to transfer our feelings onto people, we are always drawn more strongly to work with some counsellors than with others. Counselling is about our *subjective* experience, so it is impossible to choose those we work with completely objectively. In addition, if we are drawn to work with certain counsellors, it may well be that they are offering us something that we need; equally a strong negative feeling about a counsellor will make it difficult to work with them.

Before you go further, spend some time thinking about what your expectations of counsellors are and what they tell you about the kind of counsellor you need.

● What past experiences have you had of counsellors? What expectations have these left you with?

● What past experiences of counsellors have you heard about? Again, what impressions of counsellors have they given you?

- Think of how you have seen counsellors or carers portrayed on the media — on television, in books. What ideas have they given you?

- What counselling stereotypes fill you with horror, and which rather appeal to you?

All of these factors will inevitably prejudice your view of counsellors and counselling. Thinking about them will help you to make a better decision when faced with real counsellors to choose from. Once you have thought this through, consider these specific aspects of the sort of counsellor you might want.

- *Gender* To some clients, it is of vital importance that their counsellor is of a particular gender, usually the same one as themselves. They need to feel that they are talking to someone whose experience of life is, on this most fundamental of levels, the same as theirs. Equally, as one woman told us 'I'm working through having been raped at present — there is no way I could work with a man.' However, some experienced clients report choosing counsellors who are of the gender they are concerned about. With their counsellor's consent and help, they use this opportunity to work through their issues on the gender they feel negative about.

- *Culture* Particularly if you are living in a culture that is not your own, it is often helpful to choose a counsellor who shares your outlook. If you are in a minority culture, this may not be easy, but particularly if one of your main counselling needs is for support, it may be worth persevering. Similarly, you may wish to choose a counsellor who shares your social background. Nowadays, 'class' or 'upbringing' are far less important social distinctions than they used to be, but if your issues are linked with these factors, you may need to choose your counsellor accordingly. 'I felt very uneasy about my background, which was very different from that of the people I worked with,' said one interviewee. 'When I first started counselling, I needed someone who'd had the same type of Hindu upbringing that I had, and understood how I felt.'

- *Age* You may feel that you want a counsellor who belongs to a particular age group. Would you feel more at ease if your counsellor were older than you are? Would you feel more relaxed if he were the same age? Some people feel uncomfortable with or patronized by counsellors younger than they are, whilst for others, it is not an issue at all.

- *Sexual preference* If the issue you wish to work on is sexually linked, it may be relevant to choose as a counsellor someone who is supportive of your point of view. Dr Marny Hall's excellent book *The Lavender Couch* (Alyson Publications, 1985) which is addressed to lesbian and gay readers, makes the vital point that it is not necessary to have a counsellor who shares your preferences in their sexual life; it is however necessary to have one who is *affirmative* of your preferences, whatever they are and who will 'help (you) to hear and honour (your) own inner rhythms.'

- *Qualifications and experience* In Britain at present it is legal for anyone to set up as a counsellor, without any training or qualifications[3]. In fact, though, most counsellors have had some training, often in a number of disciplines, often over a long period. You may be tempted to think that qualifications and years of experience are a guarantee of a successful counsellor. It is certainly true that many experienced, qualified counsellors are very good, but we have heard of highly trained practitioners who have been of very little help, and of totally inexperienced, untrained counsellors who have wrought miracles. If you get on well with your counsellor and they are giving you what you need, this is the best qualification of all. However, as always, you need to decide this for yourself. It may help you to look through Chapter 15 which outlines various counselling schools and indicates the sort of background counsellors who work within these schools are likely to have.

What will you give?

It is a cliché to say that you have to give to receive but in the case of counselling, it is certainly true. If you are pre-

[3] The situation is changing. We have strong reservations about creeping 'professionalism' in the counselling world, since it is stifling some of the best and most original workers in the field.

pared to commit yourself to your counselling contract, you will almost certainly receive commitment back.

It is not a question of how much have you got — how much money, how much time, how much energy — but how much of each you want to give. There are people who devote a third of their income and a tenth of their waking hours to their counselling sessions. There are other people who think this behaviour the first sign of madness. Equally, what is a financial strain to one person may be a drop in the ocean to another. There is no objective value for counselling, nor a golden rule concerning how much counsellors should charge. Instead, you should think about how much it is worth to *you*, and what you might expect to get for the amount you are willing or able to spend.

Consider, for example, these questions:

● What do you want to achieve through having counselling?

● How much is achieving this goal worth to you: as much as a house, a car, a three-piece suite, a holiday, a shirt or blouse, a meal?

● Less than any of these?

● More than any of the these?

Counselling is an investment. You know how much you could or would pay for each of these items, so this gives you some idea of how much money (as opposed to other resources) you are willing to put into achieving your counselling goal. You will also need to think about what, materially speaking, you are prepared to give up in order to achieve it.

Now you know what counselling is worth to you in material terms, consider these basic issues around what you need to give in order to gain the right counselling.

Money

If you have no money to spend on counselling, then you are probably going to have to opt for NHS or voluntary counselling. A lot of counselling is done on a private basis, but this does not mean that the 'free' options are necessarily not as good. However there can be disadvantages to free counselling. The disadvantages of the counselling offered by the health service are, firstly, that counselling provision is desperately scarce and, secondly, that bad counsellors can survive within the NHS for longer than if they were in practice in the private sector. The disadvantage of the voluntary sector is that the counsellors are often under-resourced — the counselling may be superb, but the waiting room is unpainted, the admin support sadly overstretched. However, in the words of one interviewee, you may prefer to 'be counselled by an enthusiastic volunteer than by a blasé professional'.

If you have money to spend on counselling, you will need to decide how much you have to spend and how quickly you want to spend it. For instance, do you want to spend a lump sum on a weekend residential course, or pay a smaller regular fee for longer term counselling, although you may spend more in the end? It is difficult to give any guidelines on prices of sessions here, some counsellors charge £5.00, others charge £40.00 per session! The factors involved in deciding how to spend money on counselling are manifold: Do you want longer, irregular sessions rather than expensive residential treatment? Do you want to negotiate a skill swap? Do you want to opt for a less experienced and therefore cheaper counsellor?

Time

Counsellors vary widely in the demands they will make on your time. Some insist on a twice-weekly commitment for at least a year, whereas others may require a total commitment of ten sessions. The function and style of the counselling you choose will influence the amount of time it will probably take. Support-based work will usually mean you want and are prepared to give longer time commitment than, for example, information-based work. Analytical styles of counselling will tend to demand longer-term work than humanistic styles. 'I was concerned when my counsellor suggested I see him for about two months,' reported Stephen. 'I preferred to see another, more expensive counsellor who could give me a longer-term involvement.'

A final thought about time is this. An independent

research study by the Artemis Trust showed that people are unwilling to travel for more than twenty minutes in order to attend counselling or other forms of personal development. If they did commit themselves to travelling, the study showed, they were less likely to continue it. So, if you are proposing to travel more than twenty minutes away, think hard about how long you can keep up this commitment.

Other commitments

Some counsellors ask for other forms of commitment. This can vary from simply giving your real name to agreeing to stay off all forms of consciousness-altering substances, including tobacco, while you are in counselling. Some organizations, particularly those dealing with specific issues, ask of you commitments relating to those issues — following a specific diet, promising to do certain tasks each week, keeping a journal of your progress. Co-Counsellors expect you to give as much counselling as you receive. Although many counsellors make no such demands, you need to have thought through the sorts of commitment that are totally out of the question for you and the kinds you would see as essential to your development, and so happily make.

Ralph worked with a counsellor who operated a 'pay by results' system. They negotiated that if Ralph got the progress he wanted, then he would pay his counsellor £250. In the event, Ralph saw a good result after only two sessions, but felt resentful about paying over such a large amount of money when 'it didn't take all that much time.' He sent the counsellor fifty pounds only, and did not return for further sessions.

What now?

We have covered a good deal of ground in the course of this chapter, considering all kinds of topics in a bid to help you become aware of what you need and want. You might like to take the time at this point to think about what you have learned, using the grid overleaf which brings together all the topics we have raised, and now offers you an opportunity to note down your realizations.

Exploration: *What sort of counselling do I need?*

I need counselling that offers:
- *information*
- *support*
- *insight*
- *change*

It should be:
- *issue-based or*
- *generalized*

I want it to follow a particular school of thought:
- *one that has a particular style*
- *individual, couple or group*
- *residential or non-residential*

What sort of counsellor do I need?
- *gender*
- *culture*
- *age*
- *sexual preferences*
- *other requirements*

What can I give?
- *money*
- *time*
- *other commitments*

Chapter 3

How to find what you want

Tim, confused by his inability to decide on a career, decided to take counselling. He began by asking around at work, but found that most people had never considered such a step and didn't know where to start either. He ended up by using the library at his professional union to give him some leads. 'They were only names in magazines, but at least they were a starting point.'

When Jan decided that she needed to take counselling, she was with a friend at the time. 'The phone rang, and it was the counsellor that my friend had just been recommending. It was strange, and somehow meant.'

Finding a counsellor can be instantaneous or a lot of hard work. This chapter offers you a number of starting points and also a framework in which to organize them.

- We first ask you to consider what resources you have to put into the search
- Then we offer a list of all the routes we have found for tracking down a counsellor or counselling approach
- The action plan at the end of the chapter gives you space to gather your thoughts, remind yourself of your goal and think about what to do next.

What resources have you?

You need first to assess just how much energy you have to put into your search. Unless you are in an immediate crisis (in which case, phone the Samaritans) *don't* opt for the first counsellor you find in the Yellow Pages. Counselling is likely to change your life, so it is worth putting a realistic amount of time and money into finding the counsellor who will be best for you. Books, directories or phone calls to your friends are a good starting point. If you are short of money, a time-consuming but low-cost tour of local growth centres[1] or wholefood shop notice boards might be your first step.

Ways of finding a counsellor or a counselling method

The best way to use this section will be as a reference resource; try the methods that appeal to you most and, if you get nowhere, move to other methods. Remember that here, we are not yet talking about checking whether a particular method or person is right for you, only about tracking them down in the first place.

Resource books

Resource books about counselling, like this one, will often list counselling organizations. They usually give the address of the head office and to find a counsellor, you will need to contact this central branch first. Books rarely give names and addresses of individual counsellors, usually because counsellors' working approaches (and addresses and telephone numbers) cannot be relied upon to stay the same during the normal lifetime of a book.

If you read a particular work by a counsellor, and wish to contact them directly, the way to do this is through the publisher, who will forward letters on. We have worked with a number of people who have been drawn to us through our writing; they often know what to expect from us by reading our work, and we find that this helps us to get a good counselling relationship established very quickly. So please feel free to contact us if you wish!

---

[1] See Chapter 10

Telephone information services

Some telephone services, such as 'Health-line' or the increasing number of magazine-based telephone tapes, are just for listening. Although helpful, they give information only, often on health issues, sometimes on emotional areas such as 'infidelity', 'loneliness' or 'depression'.

Telephone counselling services

These are an excellent starting point if your need is for immediate support, with or without information. The Samaritans is probably the most well-known of these, but many towns have general help-lines, along with specific ones for young people or gay men/lesbians. Many organizations also offer help-lines on specific problems. As we mention later under the section 'Telephone directory', the directory or operator will help you find a relevant number. Many help-lines seem to have a system of stickers, so checking on the back of public loo doors can give you local help-line numbers!

Notice boards

Notice boards are excellent sources of counselling information if you choose to go to places where it is known that counselling is sought and offered. Health food shops, growth centres, community centres, health centres, church notice boards, libraries or evening class venues where counselling is taught are fertile ground for such information.

Large organizations seldom advertise in these venues, but individual counsellors and smaller counselling groups, often self-run, do. Your main difficulty will be sorting out the many varieties of approach offered. One of the advantages of looking on notice boards is that you get immediate information about the counsellor concerned simply from the advertisement they have placed. 'I immediately liked her for the drawing on my therapist's[2] advert; reports Jill. 'I thought that anyone with that kind of humour had to be good value!'

---

[2] We lump therapists and counsellors together in this book — see Chapter 1.

Telephone directory

Most counselling organizations list their number openly in the telephone directory, though you will need to know at least their name to be able to look them up. Some counselling networks like to keep their number confidential for a variety of reasons. For help-lines, whose actual name you might not know, the operator should be able to help.

Individual counsellors often list their names in Yellow Pages; try under *Therapy, Hypnotherapists, Psychotherapists.* This is quite handy for checking someone's geographical location. But be warned — Yellow Pages are notoriously 'shark'-infested, so do not assume that someone listed in them is necessarily good. And they don't help at all if you are looking for a particular kind of counsellor or counselling approach. Always have an initial, introductory meeting with a counsellor you find through the telephone book before committing yourself to a long-term relationship.

Professional resource lists

Nationwide counselling organizations often have lists of counsellors in local areas which they can send you. Try any issue-based organization, any professional counselling body or any training organization. The British Association of Counselling has a large resource list, area-based, giving name, contact address, some idea of each counsellor's approach and the type of clients they see, available on request from their Rugby office.

NHS

If you want counselling under the NHS, then your first point of contact will be your GP. As we mention elsewhere in this book, the National Health Service is severely overstretched, and the chance of your being able to choose from a variety of counsellors is low. If you get anywhere at all, you will probably be referred to a counsellor or counselling group at your local Health Centre or hospital, and will not make contact until the appointment itself.

Magazines

There are a variety of publications, some more 'alternative'

than others, in which counsellors and organizations advertise. These can vary from *Self and Society,* the magazine for
the Association of Humanistic Psychology, to the London
entertainment listings magazine *Time Out.* In a typical week,
there were forty advertisements for counsellors in *Time Out,*
mostly placed by individual practitioners, giving their name,
telephone number and the particular issue they specialized
in[3], but numbers also from crisis organizations such as the
London Rape Crisis Centre, and counselling training organizations specializing in such fields as Psychosynthesis and
Co-Counselling. Magazines from an organization are available by post from that organization; others can be found in
newsagents and bookshops, particularly those linked to a
health food shop or health centre.

---

*On holiday and with her young son taken into hospital as
an emergency admission, single parent Janice felt she had
nowhere to turn. She rang a local help-line whose number
she took from the 'phone book. It turned out to be a help-line
for young people, but, after listening while she expressed her
initial panic, they referred her on to a local Church befriending service. The following morning, Terry came round to take
Janice to the hospital. He ferried her round helping her
organize what needed to be done, and allowed her to cry when
she needed to. When, eventually, her son was diagnosed
epileptic, and he and Janice were taken home, Terry made a
link with a counselling organization in Janice's area and
arranged for longer-term counselling to help Janice come to
terms with her son's condition and how it was going to affect
her life in the future.*

Personal contact

Most of the clients we spoke to found their counsellors
through personal contact, usually through a recommendation from friends. Equally, most of the counsellors we spoke
to said that many of their clients came to them through
recommendation.

---

[3] Once again, beware sharks. *Anyone* not personally recommended by
someone you trust should be checked out carefully.

There are drawbacks to recommendations from friends: Sally went to her first counsellor on recommendation and found that the 'tough but good' approach that her friend talked of was for her, 'bullying — I didn't feel she cared at all.' Question your friend carefully as to exactly what she thought she got out of her counselling and make sure that what she valued is what you want too. Also, check whether you feel that what your friend said she got from her counsellor was what she *actually* got; if she says that she feels different, but you notice no difference in her crying bouts about her ex-boyfriend, be aware of this. The reverse can also apply — you might see positive changes in her that she's not yet aware of. This is evidence of a really good counsellor at work.

Going to a counsellor through recommendation means that you will have some idea of what to expect, albeit through someone else's eyes. Even if your expectations are inaccurate, they will help you overcome the first nervousness and even before you start, you will have some evidence of success to increase your confidence in your counsellor.

We also support personal recommendation because it fosters genuine good counselling far better than going by paper qualifications ever can. So the more that good counsellors are supported by their clients' belief in them, the fewer chances there will be for the (very few) sharks to shame the profession, and the less scope there will be for the (far more dangerous) bureaucrats to load the whole process down with regulations and qualifications until all the best and most innovative counsellors have been squeezed out of it.

Workshops[4]

Self-development workshops are another excellent place to find counsellors in the first place, as well as to check whether you want to work with the ones you hvae found. Many people who go to workshops are either already undergoing counselling or are counsellors themselves, so you should be able to get recommendations, or to make your own.

Particularly if you are opting for a particular counselling discipline, look out not only for names of organizations and

[4] For more on what a 'workshop' is and does in this context, see Chapter 9.

people (noticeboards, magazines, etc) but also for introductory workshops in that discipline. They will give you the chance to meet people and make contacts.

Action plan

The list of possible contact points may have sparked off many ideas for you. This final section is intended to act as a framework, or action plan, to support you in your search.

Work your way through the sections, making notes where necessary, to reach the point of having at least one counsellor whom you can contact, by using the guidelines offered in the next chapter.

What am I looking for in counselling? (reminders from chapter 1 and 2)

From this, do any counselling organizations come to mind?

What am I looking for in a counsellor?

From this, do any particular counsellors come to mind?

What resources can I put into finding what I need:

Time:
- *How long do I want to take?*
- *Is there a deadline?*
- *When can I spend time looking?*

Money:
- *How much money can I put into looking?*

Possible places to look: (collect names, addresses, phone numbers)

- *Health centre*
- *Growth centre*
- *Health food shop*
- *Church*
- *GP*

Numbers in telephone directory or other sources:

- *Books*
- *Magazines*
- *Library*
- *Bookshop*
- *People I know who have had counselling*
- *People who have other contacts in counselling*

Addresses of useful organizations

Contacts for useful workshops

Names of organizations to contact:

1
2
3
4
5

Names of counsellors to contact:

1
2
3
4
5

Chapter 4

First contact

A crunch point for many people who are deciding whether or not to work with a particular counsellor is always the first contact with him or with his organization. If they are put off, by a receptionist or even the answering machine, people don't usually take it any further — they either go elsewhere, or drop the idea of having counselling altogether!

This chapter is a preparation for this first contact, including:

- a chance to review your agendas
- a list of the types of contact you might make, with hints on making the most of each
- a check-list of things to ask your counsellor on first meeting
- a list of the counsellor's agendas
- a section on making your choice.

Your agendas

As you approach your first contact, look back at the needs you identified for yourself in Chapter 2. These are the things you hope to gain from counselling, or the issues you want to address. You will probably also have looked through Chapters 14 and 15 to get some idea of which issues and which counselling movements most appeal to you, and why. From these chapters, you will have built up a clearer picture of what you expect from the contract you are about to make. We suggest you remind yourself now of the answers you gave to these questions when you were reading Chapter 2.

What do I need from counselling?

Do I need counselling that gives me information, support, insight or change — and in what combination?

What issue, if any, am I addressing?

What style of counselling am I looking for? Does this suggest any particular approach to counselling?

Would I prefer individual, couples or group work, residential or non-residential work?

What sort of counsellor do I need, in terms of gender, culture, age, sexual preference, other requirements?

What are my limits on time, distance, money, energy, other commitments?

Now that you are ready to begin making decisions, also consider these questions.

Are there any things about an individual or organization which would immediately prevent me from working with them?

Are there any things about an individual or organization which would immediately convince me to work with them?

If you have only one person or organization to contact, your decision may be either to work with that person or not to go into counselling at all. If you have a list of contacts, you need to have some idea, which may change as you see more counsellors, of what will happen if you cannot decide between various options. Will you try one session with each person, or commit yourself for a series of sessions to one person only?

Types of contact

Letter

It is very rare for client-counsellor contact to be by letter. It has only happened twice to us in five years. It would probably work best with an information-orientated counsellor.

Telephone answering machine

Many individual counsellors are freelance and use an answering machine to take their calls while they are working to prevent them missing contacts. It can be a blow once you have steeled yourself to make a phone call to have to speak to a machine. If you have a list of counsellors to call, those who speak to you in person the first time you call may be the ones to get your business. If you do choose to persevere, leave your name and telephone number, and some indication of the fact that you are a prospective client. There is no need to outline your problem when you are talking to an answering machine. 'I need that kind of information from the person — I can't ask a machine questions,' said one counsellor we spoke to.

Telephone contact

The person you first speak to when you finally make contact may be a receptionist or secretary speaking for the counsellor. So it is not appropriate to explain your entire problem straight away but you can give a brief outline. For example, 'I'm ringing to ask if you work with depression,' 'I'm enquiring whether there are still places left in the therapy group. . .' so that the counsellor knows what you want to talk about when he or she calls you back. A receptionist can usually give you basic information on times, prices and availability, but don't expect him or her to have all the counsellor's expertise.

Your impressions of the counsellor or counselling organization begin to be formed from this very first contact. Obviously, you can't get a complete picture when you only hear a voice, but, even then, you begin to develop a relationship. As John Rowan points out in *The Reality Game*, your counselling 'has started...with the first phone call.' If your counsellor isn't aware of this, then he needs to learn it.

How does the counsellor respond to you? Does he answer your questions directly or fudge issues? 'He was more concerned with taking my booking than with finding out whether or not we could work together,' said one client we talked to. Our favourite comment on this was from one of Ian's clients, who wrote, in response to a survey, 'I liked your telephone manner. Brisk, practical, a sense of humour and straight up and downness, rather then the professionalese of many counsellors.'

Remember that, as we explain later in this chapter, your counsellor too will have agendas. He will almost certainly be aiming from the first to help you feel at ease and accepted; to begin to gather information about how he can work with you; to set the framework for your sessions together. You can help by answering his questions, and by asking him any questions which may be worrying you. Many of the agendas you will have are best discussed in your first face-to-face, meeting—but the ones that help you decide whether to proceed further need to be tackled now.

Telephone counselling

If you ring an emergency service, it is likely that the first person you speak to will be the person who counsels you. Telephone help-lines and emergency counselling services of all kinds are staffed by trained people with a great deal of expertise. They expect to spend time counselling on the phone, and are able to achieve many of the results that a face-to-face session would have. Because of this, you won't be applying any of the checks described above and it is most unlikely, in fact, that you will feel in mid-stream that you want to veto this person as your counsellor.

However, it is possible to do so if you want to. If you feel

> *Alison was starting work as a counsellor, and to do so, she placed a regular advertisement for six weeks in a local paper, giving her name and phone number. At first, she found she was having difficulty 'selling' herself when people rang. She was concerned that she would come over well to prospective clients, and often having talked to them and told them what she did and how much she charged, callers would ring off without having booked a session. She said she also found that some people just rang her number to chat or even to shout insults down the phone. It was a real baptism of fire. After a while, she reports that she started to concentrate not on how she was feeling or on worrying about what people would think about her, but on them and how they were feeling. The phone calls went better after that, she did start getting clients and making a success of her practice.*

uneasy with the counselling you are receiving over the phone, then say so. 'I realized immediately I rang (a help-line for young people) that I wasn't in the right place. I needed someone to listen, and they kept giving me advice,' reported Sally. 'I eventually broke the connection and phoned elsewhere.' But remember that a telephone counselling service cannot, by its very nature, give you what face-to-face counselling can. A telephone counsellor can't pick up *all* the signals you are giving, nor can he or she support you with touch. And, of course, it's not a route to long-term support. On the other hand, such counselling can be bless-edly anonymous—and it is there instantly.

Introductory groups or workshops

Good places both to make contacts in order to find a coun-sellor, and to check out someone whom you might want to go to for counselling, are workshops[1] or introductory groups. If you are opting for group sessions for your coun-selling work especially, you will get some idea of what their approach will be, and you may be able to see your prospec-tive counsellor in action. 'I always check out anyone I've heard good things about by going to a workshop, if they run

[1] See Chapter 10.

them. I also usually wangle it so that if they are doing demonstration counselling, I get to be the one they work with! That way I get a trial run,' admitted Jo.

Such meetings often focus on a particular approach, such as Co-Counselling or Psychosynthesis, or around a particular issue such as giving up smoking or losing weight. Sometimes they are simple talks about the approach or the issue, perhaps with slides or handouts. Far more likely is that the workshop leader will suggest some experiential work (doing and experiencing, not just talking), with simple group games, paired talking or fantasies followed by group discussion. Remember that everything is optional, and you should distinguish between the sort of activities you may do in the group as opposed to the ones you may do in a one-to-one counselling session.

Because of this, it is useful to check with the workshop leader at the end of the course how individual counselling would differ from what you did in the group. This should be a chance for you to have a brief chat with her about the possibility of doing some counselling with her particular approach, with her particular organization, with her, if that is what you want, or with somebody she recommends. Be warned, however, that at the end of such workshops many other people are usually clamouring for the leader's attention.

Face-to-face — the initial meeting

Meeting your counsellor face-to-face has to be the most satisfactory way of assessing whether he feels like the right person for you. In most cases, this first meeting will also be your first session, although in larger clinics it is more likely to be an assessment session where the counsellor decides whether to take you on himself, or to refer you to someone else in the practice who may have different skills or specializations. Obviously, this also offers you a low-risk opportunity to see whether the counsellor is right for you.

The counsellor's place of work may be at home, a clinic, or a counselling suite within the organization where he works. As you enter your counsellor's workplace, you will immediately, and quite naturally, start summing him up. Notice any evidence of the way in which your counsellor works—is there a couch or easy chair for you to relax on,

cushions for you to sit on the floor, or a desk dividing you
from your counsellor? If you are going to work in a group,
how are the chairs arranged, and what does this tell you

Questions you might want to ask your counsellor

*I particularly want to work on . . . Will you be willing to help
me with that?*

These are my goals for my work with you—what are yours?

*Would you be willing to see me alone/with my partner/in a
group?*

*What happens in a typical session with you? What sort of
things would we be doing?*[2]

*Are you happy to work with issues around (any risky material
you may want to deal with)? Are you supportive of (any
minority group you may belong to)?*

*Are you willing for me to phone you between sessions for
emergency support? Do you offer any other forms of support
(leaflets, self-help groups, tapes etc)?*

*What sort of time commitment would we be making to each
other?*

*What sort of money commitment will I be making? Do you
have cancellation fees?*

*Are there any other requirements you have before we agree
to work together?*

*Is there anything else you need to know from me before we
agree to counsel together?*

---

[2] For further information on the possibilities, see Chapter 5.

about the way the group may be conducted? 'I always check for the box of tissues,' said Mary. 'If I see them, then I know it's a safe place!'

What will you and your counsellor discuss during this first meeting? You will, in effect, be working out your contract— on an explicit level (time, money, commitment) and an implicit level (what you each expect from the other in terms of attitude, approach, behaviour). You will certainly want to explain why you have decided to go into counselling, your counsellor will certainly want to ask some basic questions to gather information. We have listed on page 57 some typical questions you may want to ask, based on reports we have had from people who have had experience with several different counsellors.

You will notice that we don't include questions about qualifications. Our experience is that, if everything else is equal, and you get on well with your counsellor, formal qualifications will be a minor issue. Also, a word of caution — some of the most impressive-sounding qualifications are the result of courses lasting two weekends, others are earned from intensive courses lasting years, but teaching the wrong thing! Some of the best counsellors are highly qualified, others, although equally good in quite different ways, are completely unqualified. That's why we don't emphasize qualifications.

Face-to-face — the initial session

An initial *session*, as opposed to an initial *meeting*, will include some formal counselling. This is your chance to find out, not only whether you feel good about the counsellor, but also whether you feel good about the counselling approach. Some counsellors offer trial sessions of perhaps twenty minutes, free of charge.

This initial session should be typical of the sort of work you will do when you and your counsellor make a firm commitment to each other. There can be problems about this however, because:

- You may be expecting miracles, and be disappointed when you don't get them.

- You may be nervous and therefore not get the most out of the counselling.

- You may worry about what the counsellor will think of you, and therefore not be able to open up about your issues.

- The counsellor may be using the time to gather information far more than she will do later, so the session may not be typical.

- You will probably work more effectively and more deeply when you have a chance to get to know and trust each other.

The opposite effect can occur, too. Les committed for three months' worth of weekly sessions after an initial experience that left him 'floating on air for three days'. However, as he told us, 'In the whole of that time the euphoria never came back. It was hard slog from then on, although still worth it in the end.'

All this said, a sample session may well be worthwhile, as the acid test of whether you can work together is usually whether you can work together!

> *Roger went for a sample twenty-minute session to a counsellor who did a great deal of body work. He reported that it was quite confusing being asked to decide right away whether he wanted to commit to more sessions, as he had only just got used to the counsellor's way of working which involved deep breathing and visualization. However he was able to say no, and go away to think about it. When he looked back on the session, he found that he had enjoyed it, though he had found it strange. He rang the counsellor up to ask some questions about what he particularly wanted to work on, and on the strength of this, committed for a further ten sessions.*

Counsellors' agendas

The counsellor, too, will be bearing certain things in mind when you first contact her. Especially if you are very down, the counsellor can seem like a god; an omniscient being who automatically knows about your problems and your feelings of inadequacy. She isn't, and she doesn't. She, too, may be apprehensive about whether or not she can work with you. If, for some reason, she feels she can't, then she will be doing you a disservice if she ignores that feeling and takes you as a client anyway.

These are some of the things which counsellors have told us they are sometimes concerned about in a first contact.

- *Setting up the right atmosphere for future meetings.* A good counsellor will create the correct balance of rapport and professionalism, so that when you meet again you will be able to work together effectively.

- *Setting up a framework so that you can understand what is happening and what is going to happen.* A counsellor may need to give you information about the way he works and what his expectations are of you. It is as important to the counsellor as it is to you that there is a fit between your expectations and what actually happens.

- *Checking out whether she feels she could work with you.* We have mentioned in other chapters problems of projection and transference. If a counsellor feels that she is reacting to you as someone from her past rather than the person you are in the present, she may choose not to work with you and refer you on.

- *Gathering information.* A counsellor will want to know what sort of person you are and what brings you to him in order to help you best. This may mean asking questions about your family life and past history, and also whether you are receiving any other help. This is not professional competitiveness, but 'an attempt not to ruin one support system by mixing it with another'. For example, we refuse to work with people on tranquilizers because our techniques would fight with the chemicals and vice versa.

- *Checking what your goals are.* A good counsellor will be aware all the time of what your personal goals are, rather than trying to force his goals onto you. So, he will need to know these from the beginning even if he knows that as you go further into the counselling process, these goals may change.

- *Making clear what she wants your commitment to be.* This will probably involve stating fees, telling you about any can-

cellation charges, discussing a time commitment and out-
lining other agreements such as not taking drugs during
the course of the sessions.

Remember that your counsellor is a human being. In the
same way that you are nervous about meeting her and coming to a satisfactory working relationship, so she may be both
welcoming and nervous when you arrive. John Rowan (ibid)
lists a number of emotions that counsellors might feel during what he calls the 'initial interview', and these include
being scared, getting confused, and getting intimidated by
the client (you!).

Decision time

Throughout the initial contact between your counsellor and
you, you will have been assessing each other. You will have
been doing this on two levels:

● *Are you meeting each other's explicit requirements, in terms
of commitment, time, money?* Is your counsellor within your
price range; is he willing to work on your issues; is he
providing the style or approach you want?

● *Are you meeting each other's implicit requirements in terms of
less obvious, maybe even unconscious needs?* Do you feel you
have rapport with him? Does he remind you so strongly
of someone else that you would find it impossible to work
with him? Do you feel that he is congruent about what
he is saying and doing? This is a far more subtle area of
assessment, and one which is impossible to deal with by
making check-lists. However it is probably the one which
will, in the end, make your decision for you.

In order to tap into this level of unconscious assessment,
we offer you this exploration. Take your time, maybe even
talking it over with a friend or someone you can trust, to
answer these questions:

What are my best hopes of working with this person (or organization or group)?

What are my worst fears about working with this person?

Can I realistically imagine coming away from my series of sessions having achieved what I came for?

If the answer to this last question is, 'yes', then you have good reason to congratulate yourself on having made a decision. If the answer is a gut level, 'no', then keep looking. If it is a, 'not sure...yet' then you probably need more information. This may be practical information, particularly if you are trying to make your decision after just a phone call. It may be that you need a clearer indication of just what your working relationship with this counsellor will be, and need to have a sample session. (If you have already had one, then you can always go back for another, although we suspect that, if this is the case, your answer should really be a 'no' either to that counsellor or to counselling in general.)

Finally, it could be that you need to negotiate one particular aspect of your contract with your counsellor. We offer guidelines on negotiation later in this book for times when your ongoing contract with your counsellor breaks down (see Chapter 7) but these guidelines are equally applicable here. In general, though, it is usually much easier to negotiate the practicalities such as time and money, and less easy to negotiate the things that may really be bothering you, such as whether the counsellor will support you or whether you will really change at the end of all this. 'I spent a great deal of time arguing with a counsellor about whether I should see her once or twice a week. When I got home and actually thought about it, I realized that my real issue was whether I should see her at all!'.

Once the decision is made, the session booked and written in your diary, there is nothing left to do except congratulate yourself on a bold step well taken, and start to look forward to a new adventure.

Chapter 5

What happens in a session?

This book makes no attempt to suggest what should or should not happen in a session — we hope that we have given you enough resources to make sure that you are getting what you need. However, it will be useful for people new to counselling if we include some indication of what to expect in a session. This chapter outlines, very briefly, some of the commonest activities or styles of counselling which you might meet.

It is common for completely different schools of counselling to use quite similar techniques within a session. Their aims may be different, their underlying philosophies may in fact be opposed; so the activities may have very different approaches, and outcomes. However, you, as the client, will be most aware, certainly at first, of what you and the counsellor are doing together — only later will you know how it makes you react and feel, and how it has helped you. At this point, too, you may discover what the theoretical background of that activity was.

How to use this chapter

This chapter lists many different forms of counselling style, explains briefly what may be involved in each, and sometimes indicates which schools of counselling use them. Remember that often the names for these ways of working may differ from one counsellor to another — what one may call 'client-centred listening' another may call 'free attention',

> *Janet had been in counselling for about eighteen months when she changed counsellor because her regular counsellor was about to give birth. Jan was working on issues around her father and how she related to him, and expected that, as usual, her counsellor would allow her to talk at her own pace, gently suggesting changes of direction.*
>
> *'I was totally amazed when this woman started suggesting I do all these new things. At first, she encouraged me to speak to my father as if he were there in the room with me; that felt very strange at first, but I soon found that I was able to say things I hadn't even suspected I thought. Later, she got me to sit in a different chair and pretend I was my father, which gave me even more insights. She was far more directive than Amy was, but she also came up with a treasure chest of new ideas. We looked at dreams I'd had, tried out different movements and what those brought to mind, and acted out my father and I fighting, with cushions. Some of it was very strange, but, mostly over the time I was with her, I was filled with anticipation — what would the next session bring?'*

and so forth. So don't take the names seriously — it is the activities that they represent which are important. Equally, remember that any good counsellor will be using a blend of these activities, moving freely and effortlessly from one to another within a session, as he thinks it appropriate, so don't bother trying to play 'spot the technique'!

You can use this chapter in these ways:

- to help you before you even start counselling to get a feeling for the sorts of activities that you might get involved in

- to enable you to decide which aren't for you and which you would enjoy and benefit from

- to encourage you to try (or suggest to your counsellor) different activities because you like the sound of what they have to offer

- to inform you if a counsellor offers a counselling style which you haven't met before.

If your counsellor offers a particular style that feels wrong for you, then first of all, give it a fair try. You may be avoiding an insight by avoiding the style, as feeling uncomfortable *may* be a sign that you are beginning to change. If, however, you realize that this discomfort is stopping you getting what you need from counselling, you should ask you counsellor to avoid that particular way of working. If this isn't possible, you may need a different approach, a different counsellor or a different contract.

'As if' work

In many psychoanalytic and humanistic schools of counselling, a counsellor will suggest that you imagine that something in your life is different from the way it actually is. Perhaps you are asked to speak 'as if' you have gained that promotion, or 'as if' your partner were still with you. This helps you to understand your issue more fully by taking a different perspective on it. The realizations this can bring up will often change the way you feel and behave even though the thing you have imagined didn't/won't/mightn't happen.

Assertiveness training

Assertiveness training is a communication skills training which enables you to state your needs and opinions clearly and cleanly without either getting aggressive or being dominated. Assertiveness training itself is a separate approach to self-development, but many other approaches use its ideas and skills to complement theirs. For example, within a humanistic session, your counsellor may ask you to pretend you are in a situation where you are not getting your needs met, and then encourage you to use assertiveness techniques to practise asking confidently for what you want.

Astrology

In some schools of Transpersonal psychology, counsellors are beginning to use astrological charts to gain further insights about the client's life rhythms and crises. This is still an uncommon counselling style.

Attention switching

When your work in a session has included feeling deep

negative emotion, it is useful to keep remembering that all is not negative. So a counsellor (or you) may suggest you 'switch' your attention to more positive aspects in your life. Equally, rather than leaving a session while feeling distressed, it is useful to 'switch' attention onto more commonplace things before attempting, for example, to travel.

Body language work
Your counsellor will almost certainly be aware throughout your session of how your body or voice is reflecting what you are feeling and thinking. One way of helping you to gain insights and to change is for the counsellor then to point out to you what your body is saying. A clenched fist while talking about the one you love may reveal hidden negativity. A sudden catch in your voice may show that there is some hidden feeling to be explored. Some counsellors will actually train you to use different body language.

Body work
This term is usually taken to mean all kinds of counselling style which involve working with body and body movement as well as verbally. Such work can include massage (q.v.), movement (q.v.) and breathing (q.v.), which all form the starting points for exploring feelings or past experiences in order to change current distress. Many varied approaches use bodywork, from Co-Counselling through to Encounter. (Any kind of counselling called something beginning with bio' is bound to involve bodywork of some sort!)

Breathing
A large number of counselling schools, such as Bioenergetics and Rebirthing pay attention to that essential aspect of your life, breathing. Some will simply point out to you that your breathing has altered in some way, and invite you to consider what that means for you. Others will encourage you to breathe in a particular way in order to enable certain memories or feelings to come back to you so that you can work on them.

Catharsis
This is another word for releasing your emotions. Sobbing, laughing, screaming, shaking are all ways of showing that

you are emotional — happy, fearful, angry, upset. Many humanistic schools of counselling encourage catharsis in the belief that emotions are better out than in. Catharsis can also lead to insight, and can get you out of the 'it's bad to feel bad' trap often found at the root of depression. Your counsellor will support you while you show your feelings, and will encourage you to do so more, maybe by giving you a cushion to hit, holding you as you cry or by using some of the other methods described in this chapter. Having permission, maybe for the first time in your life, to be as emotional as you choose may be a great release for you. In Co-Counselling, catharsis is referred to as discharge.

Don't feel, however that you have to be emotional in order to impress your counsellor, or that all counselling is about catharsis.

Celebration

Counselling is *not* all about feeling miserable, although some counsellors tend to forget this. The end point of most techniques is to help you feel better about yourself and your life. Your counsellor will almost certainly be delighted if you feel good about something you have done, thought, felt or realized. More than that, delighting in yourself is widely recognized as being positively therapeutic. In our culture, it can seem strange to be asked to celebrate something you have done; it is often regarded as boasting and frowned upon. Remember that your counselling session is a safe place to feel good about yourself, and that the better you feel about yourself, the more you will be able to feel good about other people.

Challenges

Your counsellor may disagree with you, challenging your assumptions about the world and about yourself. This can feel *very* uncomfortable; remember that a counselling session is different from a normal social interaction, where disagreement means argument. If a counsellor challenges you, she is doing the job you asked her to do — helping you to change your mind and change the way you live. Provocative Therapy is based on the idea of the challenge.

Checking out

You may be making assumptions about people which are not true. If your counsellor suspects this, she may encourage you to check out with these people what their viewpoint really is. Your perspective on the world is not the only one, and realizing this may give you insight. Checking out is a technique particularly used in group counselling, where members of the group may imagine all kinds of negative feelings from other group members, and need to be clear about this before being able to feel safe enough in the group to bring up their issues. 'Rational' or 'cognitive' counsellors are also particularly likely to use it.

Commitment

Both in one-to-one and group counselling, you may want to or be encouraged to make a commitment — such as being there on time or attending and paying for all the sessions. This is not just to enable you to know you can trust each other to be there, to be on time and so forth. Nor yet is it just to secure the counsellor's income, although this is also a factor. Making a commitment and keeping to it is part of the counselling process itself. Deciding which commitment to make, working through any difficulties you have, reaching your goal and looking back on what you have achieved are all ways of feeling better about yourself and gaining insight and change.

Confrontation

Confrontation is often used in encounter groups, but it can also be used as a tool for individual counselling. Being told clearly and with feeling what someone else feels or thinks about you can be a new and enlightening experience. Saying to someone else how you feel and think about them may give you the confidence that you can take charge of your own life. Confrontation has had a bad press because it has been used insensitively, but used wisely[1] and with discretion it can help you to face up to the issues in your life.

---

[1] c.f. The regular advertisement in *Time Out* offering 'caring and confrontative' counselling.

Daydreams

Many schools of counselling use guided daydreams as ways of getting in touch with issues and bringing to the fore realizations about these issues. Your counsellor may encourage you to relax and then suggest certain starting points to you — a journey, a message, a visit. After the daydream, you talk to your counsellor about what you imagined, and together you will analyse what these things mean for you. Some schools, such as Transpersonal Psychology, have their own ways of interpreting your daydreams and creating your own personal mythology.

Desensitization

If you have a phobia, you may choose to use a counsellor with a behavioural approach, who will use desensitization procedures to help you get used to (desensitized to) the thing you are afraid of. Perhaps you will start by imagining yourself near that thing, then seeing pictures of it, then being in the same room with it, but with a screen between you. Gradually, you will become more and more able to face the object of your fear. This technique has now been largely outmoded by quicker and gentler techniques using submodalities (q.v.)

Direct feedback

If a counsellor or a member of a counselling group tells you directly what they feel or think about you, this is known as *direct feedback*. Many counselling schools prefer to let you make your own judgements about yourself, but the direct approach can be useful in helping you to be realistic about the effects you have on other people.

Direct questioning

A counsellor may ask very direct questions for information, or to jog you into awareness of significant links between memories, events or feelings, questions such as 'What happened then?' or, 'How old were you when that happened?' This can be contrasted with open-ended questioning (q.v.).

Drawing

Particularly where a counselling school works with daydreams, fantasy, imaging or visualization, drawing may be another way to explore and express your issues and insights.

Remember that it doesn't matter a bit if you can't draw — 'being good at art' is not what it is about. Expressing what you feel or see on paper, in words, colours, shapes or lines, is. After you have done your drawing, your counsellor will spend time talking through with you what it means to you. We use it quite a lot in groups.

Dreamwork

The stereotypical activity of psychoanalysis, but it is widely used in some of the humanistic therapies too. The idea behind it is that dreams provide a window into your subconscious thought processes — hence the interest in exploring and interpreting your dreams. Your counsellor may ask you to keep a dream journal, to report any significant dreams, or identify any that have recurred throughout your life. You will be encouraged to work out for yourself, though often within the theoretical framework of the school your counsellor is involved with, what particular elements in your dreams signify or symbolize for you.

Eye contact

Your counsellor or group may encourage you to keep eye contact with them when you are speaking, in order to allow you to feel your links with others, be more aware of what is happening for you, to contact any strong feelings about other people in your life. Alternatively, you might come across an analyst who believes that eye contact inhibits your train of thought, so sits a little behind and to one side of you, so that you hear only her voice and have little interruption to your process. Some bodywork-based counselling helps you to make distinctions between different sorts of eye contact, and know how your looking is linked to your feelings.

Exaggeration

Your counsellor may help you to feel your emotions more fully (see Catharsis) by inviting you to exaggerate your words or your movements. This will help you both to get in touch with the feeling, and, often, to remember the past times when you felt it.

Free association

Your counsellor may encourage you to say whatever comes into your head, regardless of whether it seems unimportant or meaningless. This is a powerful way of beginning to realize what your unconscious mind is doing and thus gaining insight into your issues. To help you do this, your counsellor may use other styles mentioned in this chapter, such as free attention and silence.

Goal setting

It is often useful, at the start of a series of counselling sessions and during the series, to set goals for your work. Your counsellor will probably talk this through with you, and will check at certain points during your sessions whether or not these goals are being met. She may check herself whether her goals for the work are being met too. Career counselling often takes the form of a goal-setting exercise covering the whole of your life.

Grounding

Some counselling methods based on bodywork pay particular attention to positive posture. Sometimes, counsellors will ask a client to take up a particular position which 'grounds' or links them with positive energy.

Hypnosis

People who advertise themselves as using formal hypnosis aren't covered in this book, since your reasons for going to a hypnotist (e.g. to stop smoking) would usually be quite different from your reasons for seeking counselling. That said, Ericksonian hypnotherapists can be immensely subtle and effective counsellors. See also Trance.

Imagery

Counselling schools as diverse as Transpersonal Psychology and Neuro-Linguistic Programming rely on imagery as a tool for allowing a client to reaccess significant memories, develop personal symbols and myths or form fantasies of how they will be when they have changed. A counsellor may ask you to find a mental picture, maybe one that has a strong emotional connection for you or perhaps one that allows you to find a past memory. Sometimes this will allow you to listen to the sounds or voices associated with this picture. If you feel you have trouble visualizing, then you are not alone. Many people see only clouds or dark shapes, but, if they are allowed to relax, they can imagine a picture or even remember one that they have previously seen.

Inner dialogue

As with imagery, work with inner dialogue is used by many schools. Listening to your own inner voice can be a way of getting in touch with the stronger parts of yourself. Alternatively, when you inner voice is critical, your counsellor may help you to change the dialogue to one that is more positive. You can have dialogues between two or more inner voices, each representing one aspect of your personality. This is perfectly normal and a helpful way of allowing different sides of yourself to be heard. People who 'hear voices' sometimes feel as if this dialogue comes from outside themselves, often because what is being said is unacceptable to them.

Interpretation

A counsellor may offer an interpretation of why you did or said certain things, based on her understanding of it. You are free to accept, reject or learn from what she says in whatever way you choose. Disagreeing with your counsellor does not mean you have broken your contract.

Listening

Your counsellor may choose simply to listen to you. Usually, she will simply be giving you 'free attention' that is, attention where she is not judging you, but rather giving you the space to work things out for yourself without the interruptions of a normal conversation. She may also be listening for repeating patterns in your language that might give her a clue as to your mental structure.

Active listening means rephrasing what you have said and reflecting it back to you, in order to check that the listener has really understood you.

Mapping

Your counsellor might ask you to draw a map of what you are experiencing. As with drawing, this is not a test of your artistic skill, but an opportunity for you to have a new way of seeing things. Some counsellors may also show you maps or diagrams of their model of counselling, to help you understand the theory on which their practice is based.

'Mapping across' is taking a mental structure that works in one area of your life (such as confidence in your work) and teaching you to use it in another area (to create for example *social* confidence).

Massage
Some of the more bodywork-based schools use massage to enable you to get more in touch with what your body is feeling, and through this to feel the emotions around the issues that need to be resolved. Biodynamic therapy, for example, uses massage as one of its major techniques, combined with and often resulting in catharsis (q.v.) Other schools such as Co-Counselling may use massage as a supportive technique as well as one designed to encourage discharge, and many eclectic counsellors will use touch as a way for the counsellor to comfort her client.

Meditation
Although meditation itself is not a form of counselling, many counsellors welcome clients using meditative practices to find relaxation and support and some may suggest these to them. The more spiritually orientated schools may include meditation as part of the counselling process.

Metaphor work
A metaphor is a story which parallels some aspect of your life. A counsellor might talk in metaphors in order to give you more general guidance than she could simply by talking the issue through with you. For example, a story about a small child who collects all the treasures she needs in her jewel box, may lead you to realize that you have all the resources you need to have a happy life, without being too specific about what these resources are. This allows you to choose what things in your life are the right ones for you to hang on to, and which are the ones that you can let go of.

Movement
Counselling is not only about sitting and talking. Moving in a particular way may allow you to get in touch with cer-

tain distressing feelings and allow you to work through them. Moving during a session may be a way of recontacting your positive strength or your optimism. We have known counselling sessions where stretching, lying down, bending backwards and forwards and jogging on the spot were all part of the process.

Music
Some counsellors use music to relax a client during the session. Particularly if your counselling involves a great deal of regression, maybe even back to before your birth, your counsellor may like to play soft music to encourage you to feel those very deep emotions.

Open-ended questions
Questions which allow you to provide your own answers rather than needing to come up with an answer that is 'right', and which allow you time and space to explore your issue are often used in counselling. You may find this open-ended approach strange, particularly at first. When you get used to it, such questions as 'How do you feel about that?', 'What does that suggest to you?' or 'What might you do if that happened?' can be very helpful indeed.

Owning
As a client, you may be tempted to talk in generalizations, rather than about your own situation. You may be tempted to say things like, 'You always feel lonely when you're old', or, 'You can't smile at people in the street — they'd think you were mad'. A counsellor may ask you to 'own' these statements, by rephrasing them so that you are talking about yourself, and about your choices. To say, 'I feel lonely now I'm old' or, 'I feel I can't smile at people in the street' will help you to get in touch with what the real issues are for you, and so start working on them.

Psychodrama
A particular school of counselling, psychodrama is the use of large-scale role play (q.v.) to act out the situation a client may be in. In this way, the client can see her situation from the outside, but also play with it, perhaps changing parts of it, or, as 'director' of the play, having one or more people

act out different aspects of herself. It is primarily used in groups, often in conjunction with other styles of work, and is bags of fun!

Penalization

A 'technique' in behavioural therapy in which the client is punished if she fails to fulfil a task or do something she has agreed to do, or lapses back into some old pattern of behaviour. It's most often found in psychiatric hospitals, probably because no one with free choice would put up with it. Although 'legitimized' by the theory of behavioural psychology, to us it is quite clearly the stupidest way imaginable to try to help someone towards greater well-being.

Reframing

If a counsellor shows you that something you have done, usually something that you think is wrong or unhelpful, was actually positive and useful, then this is called 'reframing'. Some counsellors also use the term to refer to working with sub-personalities (q.v.)

Regression

'Regression' means going back in your memory to an earlier time, usually childhood. Many schools of counselling point out that early painful experiences are central to creating the personality problems and issues we now have, and in order to resolve these, we need to go back and heal the early memory. Each such counselling school offers different ways of doing this, ranging from deep catharsis to verbal analysis. However, they all work on basically the same principle — by changing your understanding of your early experiences you can change the way you behave in the present. Such early experiences need not be from childhood, although the most powerful ones often are. Ways of creating regression vary; a counsellor may simply ask you to 'think back', to tell her what was happening, as if it were going on right now, to speak to someone else as if they were in the room with you or use trance (q.v.)

'Rebirthing' attempts to recreate the earliest memory, birth, by allowing the client to lie in a warm, dark room, or surround herself with cushions, and by encouraging her to hyperventilate in the way that a newborn infant does.

'Regression therapy' is a term sometimes used to mean trying to go back to a previous lifetime. Obviously, this concept is only believable to people with a certain spiritual orientation.

Rehearsal

A future event may be frightening or off-putting. Using a counselling session to prepare for such an event can be very useful. Once you have counselled on the fear around, say, a job interview, it can be helpful to practise what you will say in the interview with your counsellor acting as interviewer. Very often too, when you have worked on an issue you have with a person or in a specific situation, you can end a counselling session by imagining for yourself what you will say, do or feel next time you are faced with that. From your response, both you and your counsellor can tell how you are now feeling about it. For some strange reason, this is also called 'future pacing'.

Relaxation

Relaxation techniques are used by many counsellors in many schools to enable clients to work better. They are also a major part of stress counselling.

Repetition

Especially when a client is becoming more emotional, a counsellor who values catharsis may encourage a client to repeat a particularly charged phrase or movement. This can lead to catharsis, or the very act of repeating the phrase or movement can lead to insight about, or a change in, what it means to a client.

Reward

A technique in behavioural therapy in which the client receives a reward if she fulfils a task or does something she has agreed to do. This is slightly more intelligent than 'penalization' (q.v.), but not much more, since it can lead to the client feeling patronized.

Role play

Role play is widely used in many schools of counselling, though it has been perfected and popularized by Gestalt therapists. The client imagines that a significant person in his life is actually there with him. Often your counsellor will encourage you to imagine that the 'other person' is on a cushion or chair placed near you in order to focus your attention. Often you (or someone else if you are in a group situation) will play the role of this other person. Sometimes, this can be extended to more than one player, or to imagining different aspects of yourself such as The Little Girl, or The Loving Wife (see sub-personalities). Sometimes, it can take the form of role reversal, where you pretend to be the other person, saying what you think they would say if they were there. Role play is very powerful in a number of ways: it allows you to say the things you always wanted to say, but never dared, to get in touch with feelings about others that you didn't know were there, to complete unfinished business with people who are now no longer part of your life.

Silence

In our society, we tend to be wary of silence, but in counselling situations, it is possible to be silent for a long time and feel good about it. Your counsellor may be silent because she is giving you space to think, to feel or to realize something. You may be silent because you are doing any of these things, or because you are integrating some insight or some change. It is fine to be silent for as long as you want to, and a good counsellor will respect your silence. Equally, remember that a counsellor's silence is not an indication that she is not interested in what you are saying or doing, as it would be if you were simply having a conversation with her. Instead, she is probably being silent intentionally, to help you work through your issues. The disadvantage of silence in counselling is that some counsellors can think it is 'macho' to maintain silence however uncomfortable it gets. One interviewee called this the 'the less I say, the more you pay' syndrome.

Skill training

There is a place in all forms of counselling for you to learn skills that you simply never learned before: to socialize with others, to use your body to communicate, to be assertive, to feel more deeply. Sometimes, a counsellor may offer you skill training herself, perhaps teaching you how to negotiate with your partner or to express your needs more clearly to your boss. Sometimes, she might suggest that you learn the skills elsewhere, such as in relaxation classes. One client we spoke to was told by his counsellor to go to dance classes. He did, thoroughly enjoyed it and learned a great deal about how his body (and his emotions) worked.

Sub-modalities

Sub-modalities are particular qualities of an internal image or sound[2] that can be altered to change the way you feel about something. These are things like the brightness of a mental image or the pitch and volume of a remembered sound. Sub-modalities do work, particularly a very quick and effective change technique known as the 'Swish' which is a very recent innovation, but it is rapidly becoming the workhorse technique for curing phobias and traumas, or helping to achieve specific behaviour changes.

Sub-personalities

Many counselling schools including Psychosynthesis, Neuro-Linguistic Programming, Transactional Analysis and Gestalt offer the idea that our personalities are made up of different parts or sub-personalities. This does not mean that we all have 'split' personalities; but that each of us is made up of various aspects which can sometimes disagree and sometimes work together in harmony. A counsellor working with this style may invite you to contact that part of you which, for example, wants to stay in an unhappy relationship and make it better. Following this, she might ask you to talk to that part of you that wants to make a clean break. Sub-personalities can be more archetypal than personalities and because of this you can become aware of parts of you that form the Mother, the Goddess, the Child. You can deal with sub-personalities by simply talking to them, by imaging them, or by placing them outside yourself on cushions or chairs. Such work is a way of addressing the various standpoints we all have and allowing negotiation and co-operation between them.

---

[2] The internal representations of sound, image and so-on are called *modalities*, so *sub-modalities* are further divisions of these.

Symbolism

Using symbols in counselling is characteristic of certain schools, most notably Jungian psychoanalysis. You may either develop your own personal set of symbols which have meaning for you, or work to a pre-formed set which your counsellor's school accepts. If she believes, as many do, that symbols are the way that the unconscious mind communicates with us, it will make sense if your work together takes into account the more symbolic meaning of your dreams, daydreams, fantasies and everyday life. So all objects, people, relationships and events in your life will be seen on a number of levels, including the symbolic.

Target practice

A useful term from Co-Counselling, for a style which we have found used by all kinds of counsellors. Once you have had some insight over an issue, then the counsellor may try to trigger your original unhappiness over it, and encourage you, in the context of the session, to react in a changed way. By no means as formalized or extended as 'rehearsal' (q.v.), target practice is aimed at developing new feelings and behaviours that you have discovered through your session.

Tasks

To bridge the gap between one session and another, many counsellors set tasks for clients to do. Often, these are part of the whole ethos of the counselling school, such as keeping a journal, noting down dreams, or keeping to a diet. Sometimes they arise directly out of the work done in a particular session, such as noticing the number of times you keep eye contact with friends. In couple or family counselling, you may come across paradoxical tasks such as being told to do precisely the thing you are in counselling to stop doing. To explain why this works could spoil the effect for you[3], but if you are given such a task, go with it. At absolute worst you will make no progress for another week; at best it will change not just you but your family as well. Sometimes counsellors set impossible tasks, where the aim is to learn from how you coped and how far you got.

[3] If you really want to know, read J. Haley's *Uncommon Therapy* for more insight and much entertainment, or Gregory Bateson's *Steps to an Ecology of Mind* for more insight but not much entertainment.

Thought-stopping

In behavioural counselling, when working with a client who continuously criticizes herself, or is stuck in obsessional thought patterns, a counsellor may use thought-stopping techniques. Asking the client to get into the pattern deliberately, the counsellor will then disrupt it by shouting or distracting the client.

Touch

The stereotypical analytical counsellor is someone who believes that touching a client is unhelpful. The stereotypical humanistic counsellor is someone who offers support by hugging or holding. So you pays your money and you takes your choice, so to speak! Often in regressive work, the counsellor will spend a large part of the session holding the client in order to facilitate the work.

Trance

Your counsellor may use trance to contact your subconscious directly and encourage it to change your behaviour in the ways you want. There are a great many myths about trance, and about 'hypnotism'. It is by no means an unusual state; most of us go into a light trance when we are watching television or listening to a friend talk for a long period of time. Trance is simply an altered state of consciousness where one's conscious mind is switched off and the subconscious can come to the fore.

Virtually all counselling involves trance to some degree, not least on the part of the counsellor, for example if he believes in letting you talk, and you go on just that little bit too long.

Transference

Transference happens when you begin to confuse your counsellor with other people in your life. This is not unusual — we all judge others on our past experience, and expect them to behave as similar-looking or -behaving people have done. However, this can lead to inappropriate feelings for one's counsellor — strong feelings of love or hate, jealousy or resentment. In analysis, with its relaxed schedules, transference can build up to the point where it can actually be used therapeutically. The counsellor might encourage you to become aware of your feelings about him and recognize them as inaccurate, moving on from there to discover where they came from, and how they can be sorted out. Of course, he, in turn, may confuse you with people in his past (counter-transference) and will need in turn to reduce his confusion and react to you as the unique person you are.

Visualization
Another term used for imagery (q.v.)

Writing
Writing about your issues is a common style in many counselling schools. Some counsellors may ask you to make notes on what you feel, others to keep a daily journal to mark your progress. Writing, like drawing, is simply a way of gaining another perspective on your thoughts and emotions — you do not have to worry that your writing or spelling is being judged.

Chapter 6

Sample session

In this chapter we give you a glimpse into what happens in a counselling session. If you have not been in counselling before, it offers you a reference point of what to expect; if you have, it offers a new perspective, enabling you to see and consider from the outside what you have previously only seen from the inside.

Rather than make up an 'ideal' session, we chose instead to record and transcribe a live session between Ian and Martin, a client who has worked with us before, and was happy to make public his very personal material. We wanted to give you a real experience of what a session is like, not a glamorized version. So, although we have had to edit it down to fit the space available, you still have the rambles and the blocks, as well as the leaps forward and the consolidation.

We chose to use a session that illustrates what is a standard element of many counselling schools — the information-gathering and goal-setting stage that occurs at the start of any session series. Whilst this also demonstrates many of the approaches that counsellors use — listening, empathy, reflection, questioning — it cannot give you much idea of the actual change techniques you are likely to come across. Many of these simply cannot be demonstrated in words, and in any case they vary so widely that you would be very unlikely to actully come across whatever method we used.

The commentary that Ian adds hopefully gives you an extra perspective which you may never have had before on a counselling session — the counsellor's viewpoint!

The aim of this initial session, as with all the initial sessions that Ian does, is to gain information about the client and his issue, his presented problem and the kind of solution he's looking for, and then to develop a goal for the series which is within the client's power to achieve.

Martin is a single man in his late thirties. He is going through a major career change and, for the moment at least, welcomes the uncertainty that this brings. He's fascinated by the process of counselling and has come into it looking for opportunities, rather than being driven into it by problems. He has had several sessions before, but for this session we have started afresh.

Ian   What do you wish to become?

Martin Peaceful. Calm, peaceful, relaxed, balanced.

Martin isn't in crisis — in fact his life is going quite well. In any case, the first goal he states is too large and diffuse for him to work with. So our goal for this series of sessions becomes to improve his ability to make relationships.

I   Surely you are all those already?

M   Yes, but I'd like to be more so.

I   Okay, within the context of wanting to become that sort of person, what's the most live issue for you at the moment?

M   Getting my love-life sorted out.

I   So how could that be sorted out?

M   There'd be something going on, instead of something not going on, which is how it's been for a long, long time. There would be a relationship going on with a woman.

I   When we talk about someone you care about, what's the ideal

I start trying to construct some sort of tangible goal, rather than the intangible 'get sorted out' that he has given me so far. Whatever the real problem is that he is here to work on is bound to come up when we start talking about what a real situation might turn out like.

form of this relation-
ship? In other words,
it could be based on
the idea of marriage —
though you might not
like the word 'mar-
riage' — I don't know.
But the fantasy in your
mind is that you want
a sort of marriage. It
could be that you have
a detailed and specific
fantasy, a unique
model of your own,
that would make you
happy in a relation-
ship. It could be that
you haven't got a clue,
that you haven't actu-
ally thought it through
on that level.

M   Yes, I think there is
something of a fantasy
which is a bit like a
marriage, but not with
the wife staying at
home having babies.
Not that there aren't
babies in the fantasy
but it's not a 'Janet
and John' sort of rela-
tionship. This person
would have quite an
active 'career', be out
and about doing
things, so this person
and I wouldn't be
together all the time.
There would be no,
'Hello, dear. Did you
have a nice day at the
office?' sort of crap.

*However, the answer I
get is actually stated in
negatives...*

84

I   So what would you have instead? It could be that you need to specify this from a range of options, or it could be that you have one fantasy and you want only that, or it could be that you have a singular fantasy but that you are in some way aware of limits within which it could vary.

...so I try again and this time get something a bit more specific.

M   I think one possibility is that this woman and I share very similar interests in many ways, though she has some that I don't have and vice versa, and we work together on certain projects, but not like going into the office together.

I   Supposing you found someone you were attracted to, and you set up that sort of life style, what would mark success for you in that relationship?

M   That I wouldn't get bored after about three months and end the relationship.

This is the second time that he answers a question about what he wants with an answer about what he doesn't want. I go back for more specifics about this.

I   Can I just check — is that something you have a history of doing?

M   Yes

85

I   So success would
be. . .?

M   The thing not falling
apart.

I   What I'm wondering is
whether you have
some sort of conflict
going on between
long- and short-term
criteria. Are you
perhaps setting up
relationships that fulfil
that fantasy to some
extent, and then,
because it's set up like
that, it doesn't have
the opportunity to
move on?

M   No. What's happening   *My guess is wrong*
is that my relation-   *(although there is a con-*
ships with women are   *flict of criteria). I still*
largely platonic.   *get more information*
Maybe the initial   *about the form of the*
interest was, I meet   *problem.*
somebody. I'm not
sure what it's about.
Maybe I get to develop
it into a physical rela-
tionship, maybe I
don't. I wait to see
which way the wind
blows. It doesn't blow
in the relationship
direction, so the per-
son becomes a pla-
tonic friend and that's
a repeating pattern.

I   Something occurs to   *It's important to define*
me which is that one   *what Martin means by*
of the markers for me   *success in order to have*
of a successful rela-   *any idea of what would*
tionship is the way   *constitute failure or*

that it ends. It must end in a successful way, whatever your criteria for success are. Now, the conventional successful ending once you're out of your teens is, 'Till death us do part.' Is that true for you? If it's not true for you, it might be worth spending some time finding out what would constitute a successful end.

M   I'm finding that hard to answer. Successful ending. . .yes that would be a successful ending.

I   Could there be a successful ending without one of you dying?

M   Yes, I think there could. If both people said, 'We've completed whatever it is that we need to be doing together and this relationship no longer seems to be appropriate,' and both people agreed to that, then that would be a successful ending. But in my experience, it's normally one-sided.

I   Can I invite you to step into being the Old Man?

M   On the verandah in a rocking chair, with a

success for him in counselling. It is possible that he's seeing his previous relationships as failures simply because he hasn't stopped to think what he wanted or got out of them in the first place.

The Old Man is a fantasy character that we developed in a previous session. He represents an ideal of the kind of per-

87

clay pipe.

I   If you imagine being that Old Man, looking back on a successful but consciously finished relationship, what do you most remember about it? About the relationship?

M   It's very open and the communication was very open. People didn't blame each other for things which went wrong. Lots of fun and laughter, playing; it wasn't too highbrow and serious and intense. Not intense in an *Angst*-filled sort of way.

I   What do you remember about it ending?

M   There was a celebration.

I   Still being the Old Man, how did you grow through the relationship?

M   I think through some sort of independence, not being dependent on this person for my identity, happiness and well-being; through discovering about sharing and collaboration and giving and learning.

I   How did *she* grow through it?

son Martin would like to become. He has become a personal resource that I know Martin uses to move his perspective away from present day urgency and towards a longer-term view of things. The ease and familiarity with which Martin steps into the character is what makes the Old Man such a powerful resource for him.

This is almost the exact opposite of what he said from his present-day perspective earlier on in the session. Before pointing this out to him, I want to give him a chance to firm out the idea of interdependence by thinking about what he is giving as well as what he is taking.

M   I think she learned something new about men. How you can be with a man.

I   Okay. Can I just feed back some things I've noticed. When I asked, 'How did you grow through it?' the answers, I thought, were contrasted with how you'd been in the past. Like, learning contrasted with getting dependent on her for your identity. Were you prone to that?

M   It's not just what I've been prone to, but what I see around me, this 'Janet and John' thing. Suddenly you become half of a couple. Society tends to do this to people. You become half of a double act. This is nice in some ways but there is something missing.

He says this quite heatedly. That, combined with the fact that the Old Man (also a part of him) sees the advantages of coupledom suggests that the key to resolving the problem lies somewhere in this statement.

I   So it's partly something you have fallen into yourself, and partly something you see around you, the general coupledom syndrome.

M   It's more a matter of the way other people respond when you're in a meaningful relationship. I think particularly when people

The way he slips, in one breath, from talking about other people to talking about himself suggests that he's projecting his own

89

get married, more than anything, 'married people' do certain things. It's like, 'Well, they're married now. They won't want me battering on the door saying Come down to the pub. Married people don't do that sort of thing.'

thoughts onto others. Bringing him to realize this, however, is not just a matter of telling him he's wrong. That would be both disrespectful and ineffective. . .

I   I feel you could develop the choice to step outside that

. . .but I do drop a hint. This is my first stab at restating his goal in terms of his personality — something that is also totally under his control — rather than in terms of a relationship. This is something he must share with somebody else. This is a typical manoeuvre for a change-orientated counsellor. At this stage I'm being deliberately vague about what this goal may be. That is for him to decide, not for me to impose.

M   There is an overwhelming feeling that I have with relationships, particularly with women, but also about relationships in general, that they're in danger of becoming predictable very quickly. People get to know each other a bit, and then either they're satisfied with that or

Bingo! The phrases, 'overwhelming feeling' and, 'I fear that enormously', stated as they are with some force, indicate that we have arrived. This strong, specific fear is what is blocking Martin from creating successful relationships. Since we have already discovered that the thing he is afraid of

they assume that now they know that person and it can quite quickly become cosy and a programme. I really fear that enormously	*is a projection on his part, we have now established the problem as something that is internal to him. This means that it will be within his capacity to change it, through the counselling process.*

In the next session we will work to change these blocking feelings so that Martin starts to feel that creating the relationship he fantasizes is a possible, rather than an essentially impossible, task.

Chapter 7
What to do if...

This is a trouble-shooting chapter. You probably won't want to do more than skim through it until and unless you have troubles to shoot. In it we offer:

- Some guidance as to the underlying causes of problems in counselling
- A list of common problems with specific ways to think about and tackle them
- Some generic skills you can use to solve problems.

Causes of problems

Often, problems come directly from the contract you and your counsellor have between you. This contract involves a commitment on both sides to work towards agreed goals, and some sort of agreement as to the time, money and circumstances in which this work will take place. Underlying all this, the written or explicit contract, will be an unwritten or implicit contract based on certain assumptions or expectations, for example, a certain trust on both sides that you are working genuinely, and that your counsellor is offering you genuine support, information or other possibilities.

This contract can break down in these ways.

- *Perhaps you haven't been clear enough between you from the beginning as to what this contract is, so that there is confusion, misunderstanding and consequent anger. This is likely to be* the case if your problems are characterized by phrases such as, 'I expected that. . .' or, 'I always thought that a counsellor. . .' or by feelings of disappointment from one of you and surprise at that disappointment from the other.

● *Perhaps things have changed since you first made your contract and so it needs to be remade or renegotiated.* If you feel that problems have suddenly arisen which weren't there before, you need to look at what has altered for you or your counsellor, and how this is affecting the way you feel about each other.

● *Perhaps there is a mismatch between the explicit and implicit contracts that you have.* This will occur if one of you says that you want and expect one thing but actually opts for another. 'My Co-Counsellor kept encouraging me to be open and express the anger I felt,' says Ian of an early experience of his. 'When I did, she would inch across the room away from me. Of course, I felt then that my anger really wasn't acceptable and that made me *really* angry. Then I realized that she was really having problems coping with my emotion. I was mortified, but, in fact, the problem was caused as much by her unwillingness to own up to the distress I was triggering in her as the strength of my emotions. That taught me a lot about the need for the counsellor to be honest.'

● *It could be that there is a mismatch between what you each want.* Even though you and your counsellor will have discussed your goals, a situation may arise where one of you is aiming at one thing and the other is aiming at something different. 'I don't offer my clients long-term support,' says Ian, 'I pride myself on my ability to help people as speedily as possible to the change they want, and then let them go. Sometimes they don't realize that, and start trying to see me as an integral long-term part of their lives. I even had someone block change in order to have a lever to manipulate me into giving them more time.'[1]

● *The external signs of an agreed contract are not what you thought*

[1] It didn't work. The core principle of brief counselling is that you set a maximum time limit (e.g. ten hours) at the start and stick to it. This means that you avoid the kind of dependency problems that arise in longer-term counselling.

they would be. 'I really began to resent my counsellor,' said Ruth, 'because she was trying to tell me that what I was doing was making me unhappy. In the end, I screamed at her,' 'You're here to help!' and she replied, 'Yes, but I'm not here to collude.' Then I realized that my idea of helping was just hugging me and agreeing with me, whereas she wasn't into that.' Many clients warned us that counselling did sometimes feel painful and that they were tempted to blame the counsellor for this!

● *Your contract with your counsellor starts to clash with the contracts, explicit or implicit, that you have with other people.* If other people have expectations of you as someone who is always strong, who can be relied on, and their idea of a counselling client is someone who is falling apart, they may react badly to your entering counselling at all. Equally, 'Several years ago, when I started to change, after being in counselling for a while,' said Sue 'my (then) partner got very restless. Our relationship was based on me needing him. When, I no longer did, he got frightened.' If your counselling is changing you, or making you stronger, this may affect your everyday life.

Common problems

This section covers some of the common problems many interviewees have identified. For each, we offer a description of what often happens, some possibilities as to the underlying cause, and some suggestions as to possible courses of action. The list of potential problems we offer is in no way comprehensive, and the solutions we mention are equally only a sample.

You have an argument with your counsellor

Did you in fact have an argument, or did you get angry while your counsellor stayed calm?

If the latter, you need to think about your reactions only. What triggered you to feel angry — was it something she said that struck so close to home that you felt you needed to defend yourself? If you feel that that was good counselling, and that by doing so, your counsellor was in fact showing you some area of distress or vulnerability that you need to look at, then congratulate her, and yourself, for working within your contract to take an emotional step forward. If the trigger from your counsellor was one that you felt wasn't good counselling, but was intrusive, insensitive, ineffectual, then you need to look at whether your unspoken contract of trust is still there.

Equally, if what happened really *was* an argument, with both of you attacking each other, has this altered your trust? Has it also, for your counsellor, altered her ability to work with you? Most counsellors learn, as part of their training, to be objective and stay calm even when a client is angry, so if your counsellor was joining in, this may be a sign that things are going wrong for her. In your next session, look for any signs of her unease and mention to her your thoughts and feelings about what happened — you may need to renegotiate a new contract. Even if this is not possible, it is best to be clear and clean if you want to continue working together.

Your counsellor makes a pass at you

Not mixing counselling and sexual involvement is one of the most strictly enforced tenets in the counselling rule book. *This is an absolute infringement of the contract you have between you and can be harmful on a number of levels.* It will almost certainly, in the long if not the short-term, ruin any useful counselling relationship between you because you are no longer acting as counsellor or client but as lovers, or as seducer and seduced.[2]

However, was your counsellor really making a pass at you, or were you imagining it, misinterpreting simple concern for something more? Annie told us, 'I told my boyfriend about my counsellor hugging me and he was quite concerned. I checked it out with my counsellor, who was supportive and happy to negotiate no touching if that was what I wanted. In the end, I realized that it wasn't me who felt threatened, but my boyfriend.'

[2] The technical reasons for why it is such a bad idea to have an affair with your counsellor would fill a book by themselves. Of course, if you are right in the middle of an affair with your counsellor (or client), you won't believe this applies to you. But if you have just come to the end of one, you will!

You fancy your counsellor

Because your counsellor is giving you the sort of support, help and attention that you may previously only have received — or dreamt of — from a lover, there may be a temptation to think he or she is a very special person who is particularly interested in you. This is true, but only in a professional sense. It is not unusual for clients to fall in love with counsellors, and some counsellors can handle this well and usefully — but it is a projection, and it is almost certainly something that you need to work through rather than hang onto.

A useful way to handle it would be to tell your counsellor right away that this is happening, while at the same time distinguishing between what you feel (i.e. attraction) and what you want to do (carry on counselling, rather than have an affair). This allows your counsellor either to choose to suggest you work with someone else, or to help you work through your feelings of attraction as part of the counselling process.

Your counsellor criticizes you in a way that is unacceptable to you

Some counselling methods, Provocative Therapy for example, use challenge and confrontation to aid insight and change. You may find that a counsellor who uses these methods is pushing buttons you would rather not have pushed. Here again, the contract issue is one of trust. If your counsellor makes negative comments on your behaviour, however much you resent it, you can still trust that she is keeping to the contract and helping you to make the personal change you wanted. If for whatever reason, her criticism means that you no longer trust her, then you need to either regain that trust or find a new counsellor.

You begin to feel unhappy for no reason with your counselling or your counsellor

In the course of a series of counselling sessions, you may well hit unexplained times of unhappiness or disillusionment. You can check whether any aspects of your contract, spoken or unspoken, are being broken. You can look at whether the counselling itself is bringing up the feelings without providing the means to dispel them. Particularly if your counsellor believes that the process needs to be a struggle, or painful, you may come to accept that your unhappy feelings are a natural part of your healing. 'The best thing that happened when I started co-counselling,' said Jamie, 'was finding that it was OK to cry.'

It is when you don't believe this, and start attributing your negativity to the counselling itself that you may need to think carefully about whether to continue or not.

> *Steve was concerned when his counsellor began making comments about the relationship he was in. Steve's feeling was that the counsellor did not know what was really happening in Steve's life, and he resented the fact that his relationships were being criticized. After a few tense sessions, Steve challenged his counsellor, whose opinion was that professionally he was offering possibilities to Steve which he could either accept or reject, but that he had no intention of making a personal comment on Steve's life. With this framework, Steve was far more able to be objective about what the counsellor was saying, and to consider his points calmly.*

You begin to think of your counselling session as the only highspot in the week

At first sight this may not seem like a problem. Certainly at the beginning, when you first start to pour out your feelings and be sure of being heard, to feel new understanding and change flood through you, counselling can seem like the answer to everything. Great, for a while, but if this feeling persists, without making the rest of your life seem gradually better too, then you may be becoming dependent on your counselling or your counsellor to provide you with the healing and enjoyment that you should be beginning to provide for yourself. This is not to say that you cannot get good things from counselling for an extended period of time. But the aim should always be for you to become more independent, and to be working towards a conclusion, not prolonging your counselling. This is an infringement of the contract which says that in counselling you both work towards a goal.

Your counsellor uses jargon that you don't understand

'I went to one visit,' says Carlye of her very first counsellor, 'and she drew me a little chart with words like "individuation" and "separation" on a whiteboard... that was one session and I said, "forget it." Sometimes having technical terms at your disposal can help you to understand the counselling process and feel more at ease with it. It is like being in a special club that allows you in as a member. If understanding the terms doesn't help you to feel more at ease with them, or if you can't get to grips with them, ask your counsellor either to explain what he is saying so you can understand, or not to use them. If he can't do this, look for someone who can counsel without relying on jargon.

Your counsellor puts up the price of sessions

This is something you can check when you originally negotiate your contract. 'When do you normally put your prices up,' or, 'Are you planning a price increase,' should give you warning of if and when this is likely to happen. If you have no warning, and you are unhappy about the increase, negotiate it with your counsellor.

Your money runs out

Just as a counsellor can warn you about price increases, you can make sure you can pay for the sessions you agreed to. If the money *does* run out, look carefully at your prioritization procedure — what are you spending the money on rather than on counselling? If the choice is not between eating and counselling, then you are back to prioritization. If other things are becoming more important than your sessions, then you need to look closely and honestly at why. If you no longer need or want counselling why carry on? 'I used our huge new mortgage as a reason to stop seeing my counsellor,' said Sally. 'Then I caught myself planning a holiday and thought "I need this holiday more than I need my sessions!" That taught me a lot.'

The counselling is taking longer than you expected

Ask yourself why this is. Was your counsellor initially clear with you about how long it would take? Is he now pressing for sessions when you are not sure you need them? (This is a common bad habit among independent counsellors. It's quite understandable — counselling is a tough way to earn a living — but it's not excusable.)

Perhaps you have an agenda about continuing. Look at this carefully, and ask yourself if you are breaking your counselling contract by hanging on to the relationship longer than you need to. Counselling works to a conclusion — you can always come back later, when you have been independent for a while.

You keep going to sessions late or cancelling them

Almost every counselling contract is based on giving and receiving time, and if you consistently break this contract, you need to look closely at why. We always challenge persistent lateness or cancellation, not only because we get annoyed and feel unvalued (which we do), or because we can lose money (which we can), but because it often turns out that the client is ready to stop — or has issues which need to be worked on. If your counsellor is consistently late or cancels, challenge him too.

Other people in your life feel threatened that you have sought counselling

Ask yourself why these people are threatened. If their experience of people who are in counselling is that they are 'off the wall' then you need to reassure them that you are not. Remember that counselling is a sane way to get help for problems and it is a sign of your own maturity that you are able to do so. Alternatively, 'My friends complained that I should have trusted them with my problems,' said Maria, recovering after a broken relationship. If your friends feel the same, explain that they give you things a counsellor can't, but that, equally, a counselling relationship offers complete objectivity, a relationship without history and a one-way flow.

Perhaps more crucially, your family may well feel threatened. The most usual form for this to take is that they support you to take the first step, but shortly after that begin to sabotage your progress. We have dealt with this separately in another section.

Other people in your life object if you consider stopping counselling

If other people in your life are also in counselling, they may feel that it is part of being a complete human being to be working on yourself. If you stop altogether, or change counsellors, they may feel threatened. If you secretly agree with them, ask them for their support to help you re-enter a counselling relationship. If you don't, remind them that part of any counselling contract is integration and that at present you are integrating your previous piece of work.

Other people in your life get very distressed shortly after you begin to find real benefit from your counselling

'One of the things that changed for me when I started counselling was that I wanted more time to myself,' said Jenny, a mother of four. 'My children fought that, tooth and nail.' You may get any of the following reactions from those around you when you embark on a process of personal development: anger, abandonment, accident-proneness, illness, sulks, nagging, increased demands, hysterics, depressions, tears, appeals to outsiders. Everyone in your life has some sort of investment in your staying the same[3] even if for the best of motives; friends or partners may have enjoyed your dependence, colleagues may want their scapegoat back. Therefore, other people will all, in some way, resist your counselling involvement. Why does this happen? While most of their goodwill is firmly on your side, some part of their personalities is afraid that, when you change, things will be different. You may stop loving them, you may not give them as much attention, you may not be the same person.

[3] For more on this, read Eric Berne's brilliant *Games People Play.*

You have three options. Firstly, you can stop counselling. If the pressure from outside is so great that you have to choose between your marriage and counselling, you may well choose your marriage. Secondly, you can continue with the counselling, but stop changing. Particularly if you have completed sessions and are attempting to maintain the changes you have made while carrying on with your normal life, you may, without realizing it, slip back into old habits. The third and to our mind only fully satisfactory option is to use your counselling to help you through your other problems. A good counsellor will not undermine your relationships and will give you the resources you need to increase your capacity to love others and love yourself.

That said, it is only fair to warn you that counselling *can* push you over the edge of a stale relationship, and into divorce. Is this wrecking your home or saving your sanity? It's impossible to say, but do remember that the threat to people near you may be more real than you think.

When Denise and Chris split up, Chris suggested they go for counselling in order to heal the rift. The counsellor they went to listened to them both separately and warned both that he was not prepared to work to get them back together if that seemed to be inappropriate for them. After three sessions, Denise said very clearly both to Chris and her counsellor that she was now determined to separate formally and wished to use her counselling time to help her to cope with that. Chris was furious and withdrew from counselling, accusing the counsellor of manipulating the situation, and driving them apart. Denise continued to work with the counsellor on her own issues of independence and her grief and uncertainty about splitting up. Denise and Chris are now divorced.

Your counsellor wants to stop the sessions or move you to another counsellor

We deal with this issue more fully in Chapter 9. Your counsellor's reasons for stopping may be many and varied, but the bottom line is that if she genuinely feels that it is not appropriate for you to work together any more, then she has done the best thing in opting out of the contract.

You don't like the results you're getting from counselling or you don't feel you are getting results at all

We deal with this issue more fully in Chapter 8. Remember that you can talk this through with your counsellor, and may well get reassurance that she can see changes you can't — or that she is aware of a structure to sessions that you are not.

Skills to solve problems

We have mentioned many of the skills clients use to solve problems during the previous section. We will now explain them in full and add more.

Clarify the contract

If you are unsure of what you or your counsellor is doing, or suspect that one of you has changed your mind about what the contract between you actually is, take time to clarify it.

First of all, clarify it with yourself. If necessary, write down again what you expect from counselling and what you expect to give. If this has changed from your original contract, and you think this may be causing the problems, let your counsellor know. If you went to her with a need for hugs and now you need lots of challenge, it's unfair to blame her for not meeting your needs!

Once you are clear, think of your counsellor. It could be that when you have explained to each other what your expectations are, things can be resolved. Remember that this doesn't only mean checking the explicit contract so that it is clear and agreed, but also swapping notes on your implicit contract so that it is brought out into the open. A useful exercise to do here, if your counsellor agrees, is to share with each other your expectations, beginning perhaps with the phrase, 'What I expect of you as a client is. . .' and 'What I expect from you as a counsellor is. . .'. When Lesley tried this, she 'realized that I expected my counsellor to *tell* me how to cope with situations, whilst he didn't see that as part of the deal at all.'

If you find that now, your counsellors expectations and yours don't fit, negotiate or leave.

Clarify your goals

All that we said about contracts applies to goals. First, check out your goals for yourself. They too may have changed since you first started counselling. If you feel that your counsellor's goal are different from yours ('I didn't need to get angry, I needed to decide...') then challenge him. If you feel that what your counsellor is now doing is not going to get you there, then think about changing counsellor.

Check out your trust

Ask yourself occasionally whether you still trust your counsellor. If you find that you are holding back on thoughts and emotions, if you think that he will criticize or think worse of you for what you say or do, ask yourself if this is a positive relationship to be in. If you flourish under these conditions, so be it. If you are beginning to dread your weekly session, challenge what is happening.

Check out your transference

Check out regularly if your feelings about your counsellor are getting confused with feelings about other people in your life. If they are this is not necessarily a bad thing ('I used her as a "good mother" for about eight months, and it was wonderful...'). However, being aware of it, and maybe talking about your realizations with your counsellor, may help you distinguish between any worries you have about your sessions that need to be regarded lightly and any that need to be taken seriously and acted on.

Counsel on problems

Using your counselling to deal with your problems *about* counselling can be a positive thing to do. When the problems are caused by other people in your life who are making your counselling difficult, your sessions may provide a time and space when you can let out your feelings safely. When these feelings are about the counsellor herself, then it can be more difficult. We feel that being honest about personal feelings, with an awareness of how they can be influenced by transference, can only be useful.

Negotiate

Negotiation is a refined skill in itself and we are not going to attempt to give you a complete summary of it in a few paragraphs. Equally your counsellor may not know about negotiations — he is a human being too and may not have had the advantage of reading this book! However, these pointers may help you negotiate with your counsellor for what you need.

● Negotiation is about communication and respect. You as well as your counsellor have a right to this respect.

● Negotiation is about communication. If you start getting angry with each other, stop negotiating until you feel better. If you continue to get angry, you are probably beyond having a counselling relationship.

● Negotiation is not about compromise so that neither party is happy. Negotiation is about finding a solution that satisfies you both.

● Negotiation is not about beginning with where you disagree and trying to find a solution. It is about finding a point of agreement and working down from that.

● Don't assume that you will come to agreement. Always have in mind what is your next best alternative to reaching agreement.

Further excellent guidelines on general negotiation skills can be found in Ury and Fisher's *Getting to Yes* (See Bibliography).

Leaving

We may seem to have suggested in this chapter that the answer to any problem in counselling is, 'When in doubt, leave.' In the most cases, in fact, you will be able to resolve your problems and continue counselling satisfactorily. However, we have stressed the possibility of leaving because often people forget it. They forget that the counsellor-client contract is, like many others, a voluntary one. If you are not satisfied with the results, you can stop using the product. We believe that if the knowledge of being able to withdraw from a contract is used sensitively and responsibly on both sides, then it can only result in a better, a more useful and effective tool for personal development.

Chapter 8

How am I doing?

Any consumer ought to be able to judge whether the product they are using is a good one. So this chapter is about judging the product, and all that that involves. This chapter offers guidelines as follows:

- An outline of the problems in accurately judging how successful your counselling is
- Some examples of ways in which your counsellor may judge success and progress
- Some guidance and examples of ways in which you can judge success and progress
- An exploration to help you think through the issues involved for you.

We suggest you read through this chapter after you have been counselling for a few sessions, and again at regular intervals after that. It is important to keep monitoring what is happening.

How can you judge

Unlike a fridge, a counselling contract has a variable function and every single counsellor and client will have their own particular definition of what counselling means. This is why we dedicated so much time and space at the start of this book to helping you work out what you wanted.

Equally, whilst it is easy to tell whether a fridge is working or not, it is not quite so easy with counselling. These are some reasons that our interviewees identified for finding it hard to judge whether their counselling worked:

● *It is often hard to tell whether you are achieving your goals until you have been counselling for a while.* Particularly if you expect your counselling to take a long time, you may feel that it is unfair to judge the results of sessions on just a small sample. Counsellors may well spend the first few sessions simply gathering information, so you may not see any real results for a while, but then everything may happen all at once.

● *You may feel bad about the counselling, but good about the results of it.* Some clients reported finding their counselling intensely emotional, and they didn't feel good about this at first, but if they stuck with it, they often then reported real benefits.

● *You may feel you are getting your goals, but other people in your life may disagree — or vice versa.* 'I felt really good about the counselling, but my friends told me that I was getting very self-centred,' commented Rachel. If this is happening to you, look back at Chapter 7 and the comments we make about how your self-development can affect others.

● *It can be when you feel most stuck, disillusioned or ready to quit that you get the result you've been waiting for.* It is difficult to judge any dynamic process such as counselling by a view taken at one point in time. A few sessions later, you may feel very differently.

● *Counselling is not only about the sessions, it is also about what happens afterwards.* We have sent clients away to 'integrate' their work to the accompaniment of heartfelt pleas that they 'weren't finished yet'. Some changes and insights need time to bed down into your everyday life before you really start seeing the benefits.

● *Your counsellor may be seeing things about your progress that you just don't notice.* We will expand on this point in the next section. Suffice it to say that whilst you are the consumer, your counsellor may be seeing things you don't see and so may consider you to have made very different progress from the progress you think you've made.

- *You are the last person to notice change.* Time and again, clients will come to a counsellor with a heartfelt problem, once it is resolved and in the past, it is just that — past; gone and forgotten. You may literally not remember, in the contentment of your post-counselling life, how desperately distressing your phobia, trauma or depression was to you.

All these difficulties need to be taken into account, but once they have been, there are ways of assessing just what progress you have made. One is to check with your counsellor, the other is to develop ways of checking for yourself.

Your counsellor's viewpoint

Particularly at the start of counselling, you will almost certainly be drawn into your counsellor's model of what progress is and how it should be measured. Later, you may develop your own measuring system, but can usefully check with your counsellor as to how he sees things.

Different counsellors working with different counselling approaches have different ways of charting progress — and, as most of the counsellors we talked to mixed and matched approaches, it is impossible to give a guide to how a counsellor will respond when asked how you are doing. However, we noticed when talking to counsellors (and clients) that many of them worked from a general framework against which they measured progress. Here are some examples.

- *'Things will get slowly and steadily better.'* A counsellor who works from this model of counselling will expect you to make immediate progress, though in small ways, and will be very aware of the progress you are making. She will see sudden bursts of insight or change as good, but will want to see if they last before she believes in their reality.

- *'A sudden insight will resolve everything.'* A counsellor who believes this may give you messages that everything is fine even when you are worried that you are not making progress. He holds that the breakthrough is the essential piece of counselling, and expects radical change when, and only when, this happens.

● *'Two steps forward, one step back.'* This counsellor will be particularly supportive if you suffer setbacks when you are counselling. She will expect them, and build time and energy for them into her counselling. If you do well, she may warn you to expect a reversion before you can do well again.

● *'It all takes time.'* Particularly in the psychoanalytic schools, the presupposition is that all good work takes years. We have stated our doubts about this position elsewhere; if you do work with a counsellor who holds this viewpoint, then be prepared for a long wait before he accepts that you have got your goals.

● *'Immediate change or bust.'* This counsellor will expect to make some progress immediately you begin working with her. If this doesn't happen, she may well suggest you work with someone else. This is because she believes that you will then not expect to succeed with her, not because she regards you as a 'bad' client.

● *'It will get worse before it gets better.'* A counsellor with this belief will expect you to feel bad, or your symptoms to increase, before you start to see improvement. Often he will judge you to be making real progress while you are complaining that, in fact, you feel more unhappy than before.

● *'You never really change or make progress; counselling is a lifelong maintenance activity.'* Counselling *can* be a life-long commitment, but we feel that linking that with a 'never' belief is very harmful. A counsellor who believes that (mercifully, there are few) needs either urgent counselling herself or a holiday in the Caribbean.

To show how these differing views work in context, we offer you four actual case studies of how counsellors do measure progress and success and how that ties in with their belief systems about their work and their clients. You can use these to begin to build up a picture of how your counsellor is working and how this compares with your ways of judging progress.

Ian is a brief counsellor, which means that he limits the time he will spend with each client, and also that he works to a specific brief from each client as to how they want to change. In his very first session with a client, he will spend time finding out how they want their own behaviour to be different by the end of the series. His eventual test of success will be whether this goal has been reached, but along the way he will look for interim evidence such as whether the client has any insights or realizations about the problem, or whether their feelings about the issue have changed.

Sue facilitates groups and workshops. Her aim is to help people improve their self-esteem through self-exploration and the chance to share the results of that exploration with each other. She believes that, given validation and support from the rest of the group, participants will at some stage 'get it' — make a sudden breakthrough into realizing that they too are valid, lovable human beings. The evidence of this breakthrough that she looks for is mainly non-verbal; people's body language will change, they will look around more and make larger and more confident movements. They will also smile more and communicate more with the rest of the group.

John is a careers counsellor who gives people support to change or develop their career by providing them with questionnaires to learn about themselves. He believes that having more information about oneself makes it possible to find more fulfilling employment. John would expect to spend perhaps three or four sessions in total with any one client, working through and analysing the questionnaire. He rates progress by the insights which a client reports back to him, and the new information which he can give them about their personality and career style. He is not charting progress by emotion or by change in day-to-day behaviour. Ultimately, John aims to give his clients better employment; he rates eventual success by the way clients change their job position, and the increased satisfaction which they or their employers report back to him after this is done.

Helen works as a counsellor in an NHS health centre. She works from a number of models, but believes that counselling generally takes time, and that the way she can help is to provide total acceptance of a client. She begins by spending a few sessions talking through problems, before beginning to ask more challenging questions. She feels that when clients express a new insight, this will usually herald a change in the way they cope with the world. She accepts it when clients show emotion, but in general sees progress as being made when a client is able to step back from his problems and feel better about them. Helen expects progress to be slow and erratic, and rides with any setbacks that clients go through. Helen's measures of success are when clients express readiness to go on to the group sessions, and when she hears them report increased self-esteem, or some shift in their life situation which has previously been a problem.

As you read through and learn from these case studies, you are bound to wonder at the differing beliefs and expectations of different counsellors. Surely, one is right and the others wrong? In fact, this is not the case. The subtlety with which the human mind works, the subtlety with which, in the case of counselling, two humans minds work together, means that there are many different models of progress and only you will know which are right for you.

What can be learned from the examples we gave above is this: if you check your progress with your counsellor you will get an answer based on her criteria. If this is the answer you want and the one that fits with what you feel, then this is fine. If you get a different answer, look closely at how your counsellor is judging the situation. If you are (mistakenly) working from a belief that progress is measured by the amount of pain you feel in counselling, but your counsellor expects an immediate improvement then her response will be different from your own.

In general, clients tend to believe in their counsellor's model of the way things work, because they accept that the counsellor has expertise and because they are usually drawn to a counsellor with complementary views to their own. But if you do find that your counsellor is approaching your progress with very different views from yours, you may find that though your goals are the same, the means you want to use in order to reach them are incompatible.

Your viewpoint

How can you begin to judge for yourself how you are progressing? We would suggest that one way is to check back to Chapters 1 and 2 and look at your original list of agendas. To what extent did you then want information, support, insight and change — and to what extent are you getting them?

The following notes give you more guidance on how to judge progress towards your goals in each of these areas.

Information

It is usually quite simple to check whether you have received the information you wanted. Did you get the facts, the names, the numbers? Do you now know who to approach about that job? Do you now know how to approach a woman socially, or to ask the shop to replace your washing machine in a way that will get action and respect?

Less easy is to decide whether the information you received has benefited you; it is only in the context of how it has helped that you will be able to tell whether the information is useful. So deeper questions to ask may well involve other goals on your list: did you make the changes necessary in order to get the job; did you get the insight that men *can* approach women socially, did you get the support to feel you had a right to trouble the people at the washing-machine shop?

Support

Support-orientated counselling is all about feelings. This makes keeping track of your progress quite difficult, because feelings are notoriously hard to remember accurately. (Remember that brilliant rock-climbing holiday? It wasn't — you were scared rigid the whole time.) The best way is to keep a diary which concentrates on your feelings from day to day. It should only take five minutes to write up every morning or evening, but you will find it an invaluable tool for charting progress.

Another difficulty in assessing support-based counselling is that support comes in various forms, and you may need to check that you are getting just the support you need. Have you been listened to enough, have you got the physical support you wanted? Did your counsellor help you to feel accepted — or did she challenge you sufficiently in a way that let you feel stretched?

In emergency counselling it's easy — has the panic subsided? Can you take action on the immediate problem?

In longer-term counselling, the key question to ask is whether you are beginning to *feel* the need for support less? For in support-orientated counselling it is actually possible to go backwards, by becoming too dependent on your counsellor. If, as the sessions progress, you begin to need her help in order to live your life, then this may help you to feel better — but your counsellor will detect the warning signs and may suggest that you change direction or even counsellors for a while. 'It was when I started wanting to ring my counsellor every day that she objected — and I came to realize that what I wanted was a friend, not a counsellor', said Stephen.

Eric went to a brief counsellor to work on the anger he felt towards his partner. The counsellor suggested he have six sessions, but at the end of the first, Eric felt that in fact no good had been done. When, in the second session, he spoke to his counsellor about his feelings, the counsellor said that he had noticed changes in the way Eric was behaving that suggested that in fact Eric was deriving benefit from the sessions. Eric stayed with the contract as he saw it and went along for all the sessions, but feeling more and more resentful each time. He did not renew the contract and his counsellor did not suggest that he do so.

Insight

The realizations gained through insight-orientated counselling will often be sudden and spectacular, and are quite likely to be accompanied by strong emotion. In that sense, progress is easy to test.

Powerful insight is either there or it isn't, and if it isn't you will have to decide how long you are prepared to go on before trying a different avenue. It is well worth your while discussing this with the counsellor at an early stage in your relationship. As a guideline, our rule of thumb is that four one-hour sessions are enough. We usually refer clients who haven't gained a significant insight into themselves in this time to someone else.

The other marker for success is whether this insight leads on to change in your behaviour or feelings, so...

Change

We have stated elsewhere that we believe that the underlying goal of all counselling is change. So it follows that you will want to check your progress in terms of the changes you have made. As mentioned earlier in this chapter, this may be difficult.

All counsellors have had clients who staunchly refused to admit that the counselling had helped, despite the fact that all around them, people were congratulating them on their success. It is very easy to think that 'the situation' has changed, that 'it was never as bad as all that' or 'I just grew out of it.' An experiment done with glasses which made the wearer's view seem reversed proved that if worn for long enough, they caused the eyes to adjust to the new world view and see the world normally again. The changes brought about by counselling can have the same effect.

A second difficulty in keeping track of your progress of change is that the goals alter. If you are changing yourself, your aims in the world will change too. It may originally have been vital to get into a size 18 dress but eventually your aim will be to accept your body and love yourself. Being civil to your boss may be all you can hope for at first, but eventually you may aim to understand and support her.

Again, we recommend that you keep a short diary over the course of the sessions, and for a couple of months afterwards. Note your feelings and behaviour, especially your behaviour in the 'problem context' that you have identified. Periodically, check back to your early entries. If you can't believe it was you who wrote them, you have changed.

The final difficulty we would identify in keeping track of your progress of change is one we have examined in Chapter 7. It may be that you are changing wonderfully, building up your self-esteem, allowing yourself a much more fulfilled life. But this may rock other people's boats, and so at first, your life may actually be more difficult. Be prepared, as the boats rock, for negative reactions which may tempt you to think that your work has all been for nothing and that you are still getting nowhere. When counselling couples, we always look forward to the big row, the 'shakedown' in which the things that need to be said, finally are said, as the first real sign of progress.

Exploration

To gather together all the information you need to assess your progress, we offer this exploration, which you can fill in at relevant points during your counselling.

Date

What were my original goals?

What are my goals now?

How does my counsellor feel I have progressed? (ask her)

How do other people see it? (Choose ones who are not too close to you but who see enough of you to monitor your progress.)

Do I have any objective evidence? (Such as weight loss, drop in alcohol consumption, increase in number of parties invited to)

How do I feel I am doing with respect to each goal?

The bottom line is this. If you are happy with your progress, keep on doing what you are doing. It works. If you are not happy, then talk it through with your counsellor. If you trust her, carry on. If you don't, then make a change.

Chapter 9
Stopping

Whether your experience of counselling so far has been good or bad, whether to go on or to stop is bound to be a live issue for you. If counselling has got you nowhere, you won't know whether to leave or whether to stay and hope. If it has benefited you, you won't know whether to set new, higher goals and continue, or whether to stop now. Nor is the decision limited to either stopping or continuing. There are also a number of 'sideways leaps' that you could make; into another form of counselling, into workshops or counselling groups[1] or actually into training to be a counsellor yourself[2]. But the first question is; why stop at all? 'I felt I'd found a useful tool for living; I didn't want to give it up,' said one client we spoke to. If this is so, then move on now to the next chapter. The majority of clients, however, see being in counselling as a temporary phase in their lives. If this is true for you, then at some stage you will have to make the decision to stop. Some of the issues you are most likely to be facing are listed below.

- *You feel that you are not getting anywhere.* The question here is, How long you should give it before you decide to go elsewhere? Most counsellors will have already asked you to make a minimum commitment of the time they think it takes to make significant progress. Assuming you agreed

[1] See Chapter 10.
[2] Covered in Chapter 11.

to that in the first place, we think that this is your best guide, too.

Sometimes a counsellor will argue at that point that you still need more counselling, and especially if you have already invested a great deal of time and money, there is a strong temptation to go along with this. The key decision factor here is, Do you, at gut level, trust her? If you do, stay with her. If you don't, leave — you are highly unlikely to make progress with a counsellor you don't trust, however long you stay.

● *You hit a practical problem — money, time, moving away, etc.* If the problem is genuine, and not just an excuse to yourself (in which case, counsel on it), then you have to stop. However, you can move to a cheaper or more local counsellor, or a free service. Browse through this book, particularly Chapters 14 and 15 for ideas. It can also be useful to do a prioritization exercise: what is less valuable to you than the benefits of counselling, and what is more?

● *You are dissatisfied with your counsellor or the counselling process.* Is your dissatisfaction temporary or long-term? If this has only developed recently, think before you leave — counsellors are just as capable as you are of getting out of bed on the wrong side two sessions in a row. Your dissatisfaction may in fact be resistance to facing some particularly painful feelings or memories, in which case, once again, you should stay for several more sessions. If, however, you have remained dissatisfied for some time, it is probably time to move on.

● *You have reached your goals.* Congratulations! Now that you have a taste for the process, you should consider what else counselling might get you. If you can imagine promising possibilities, consider more sessions with your current counsellor as one of a range of options. Otherwise, stop now.

● *You want to stop, but are scared of the possible consequences.* You have probably become dependent on your counsellor. Lucy found this. 'When my counsellor mentioned for the first time that I was 'nearly finished', I actually felt myself panicking.' Counsellors who work long-term know this phenomenon as 'separation anxiety', and may spend several months preparing you to make the break. Plan an ending with your counsellor and work towards it. If this doesn't work, change counsellor to someone with a shorter-term orientation, or switch to a group.

There is one other reason for stopping — your counsellor could be the one to end the contract. This could be for practical reasons, such as moving or changing jobs, the conclusion of a fixed-term contract, personal reasons such as having fallen in love with you (it does happen!) or because, in his professional judgement, it's best for you. This again could be because you aren't making progress, because you are getting overdependent, or simply because you stir up negative feelings for him[3] and he can't handle it. 'I have stopped seeing a client because of personal issues,' said Sarah, 'I counselled on it myself with my supervisor for weeks before making the decision.'

If your counsellor tells you it's time to stop, the first thing to do is find out why, since this will give you the information you need to take the next step. It is generally not a good idea to try to talk him out of it; an unwilling counsellor won't be much good for you. Instead, use him as a resource to help you plan your next step. If your counsellor wants to stop, we can almost guarantee that you will be able to find a better deal elsewhere.

Making the decision

Having taken all the above factors into account, you may well be left still saying 'Yes, but...'. It's time to trust your unconscious. Consider this one, simple, question. Take your time to answer it, noting down any images, words, thoughts or feelings that come to mind.

How would I feel if I left counselling?

Now check your responses.

● If your overall feeling was one of sincere relief, if the images and words were of freedom and relaxation, you should have left counselling a while ago.

[3] For more explanation of this, refer back to the sections on 'transference' in Chapters 2 and 6.

- If your overall feeling was one of panic, if the images and words were of being bereft, you are dependent on counselling, and should consider constructive ways to break free of that.

- If your overall feeling was one of a clear sense of closure, it is time for you to move on, perhaps to come out of counselling for a while, perhaps to begin again with a new person or approach.

- If you feel somehow (but not desperately) concerned by the thought of leaving, with a sense of unfinished business or slight loss, you need to continue with your counselling until you have achieved your outcomes.

How to stop

It is important to end your contract on the right note, not merely out of courtesy, but because bad feelings about your counsellor could inhibit you from integrating the work you have done with her into your life.

Here are Sue's guidelines for a successful conclusion to a counselling relationship:

- Clear, clean communication about the ending
- Leaving feeling good about each other, no dependence, no anger
- Knowledge of which outcomes had been achieved and which not
- Recognition of each other's contribution to the contract
- Knowledge of when, if at all, further contact will be made — for example, for a follow-up session
- Any practical information that either party needs, such as contacts in another area or an up-to-date address for mailings.

Many clients we talked to reported a real sense of loss when they stopped counselling. Whether stopping meant for good or for a while, they felt abandoned, wary, or just simply at a loss. Particularly if your counselling has been a large part of your life for a long time, suddenly being without it can be 'strange... like losing a friend. I once set off on the journey to my counsellor's home one Wednesday as usual, before realizing that, actually, we'd stopped now.'

If this happens to you, possibly because you and your counsellor have not, for some reason, been able to bring the sessions to a satisfactory conclusion, set up a closure process for yourself. Without simply replacing the counsellor with another counsellor-substitute in the form of a friend or relative, take some time with someone close to you to talk through any issues that are left unresolved.

- Explain to your friend anything that you really needed to say to your counsellor
- Imagine what it would be like having your counsellor say to you all the things you would have liked her to have said
- Think forward to a time in the future when you have worked through the unhappiness and imagine what life will be like then, the way you will feel both about yourself and about your counsellor.

When Sally went to Jennifer for help with her depression, she got a lot out of the first session. During the second session, however, she began to talk about her partner's infidelity. Jennifer listened silently and offered handkerchiefs, without passing a comment. After the session, Sally felt as if she had told Jennifer something about herself which she hadn't wanted to share, and which had not been received sympathetically. She was too embarrassed to go back again, rang up and cancelled her next session, then went instead to another, more openly supportive therapist. A few months later, talking to the friend who had originally recommended Jennifer, Sally realized that she had never really finished off her 'business' with the counsellor. She arranged to see Jennifer again, for a meeting rather than for counselling. They talked through what had happened, and Sally became clear both that Jennifer had offered the best she could and that she had needed something other than Jennifer could offer. Both of them felt better that Sally had done this, and Sally realized that her counsellor too needed closure on what had happened.

It is, however, far more likely that you and your counsellor will have prepared for stopping by coming to a real sense of closure before the break. The months after completing counselling may well be busy and fulfilling, integrating the work you have done, perhaps completing tasks that your counsellor has set you, certainly celebrating the completion of a particular, very important time of your life.

Chapter 10

What next?

Once you are no longer in counselling, what next? Obviously, you could simply close this chapter of your life and leave it at that. Remarkably few people do this in practice, probably because the journey of self-discovery, once embarked upon, is just too fascinating to stop.

This chapter covers:

- Resuming counselling, perhaps after a break, and perhaps in a different format.
- Your other alternatives — particularly the intricate network of counsellors and counselling-related activities known as the Growth Movement.
- An exploration to help you focus on whether and how you want to use counselling in the long-term.

Resuming counselling

It could be that the unhappiness or symptoms that originally drew you into counselling have returned. If your issue is concerned with your relationship or your family, you may have found that other problems have occured as a result of the changes you made.

Counselling will have aimed to give you the resources to change the situation completely, but, as we have said before, if external circumstances are too strong for you, this may not happen and you may slip back into your previous unhappiness. If this happens, remember that neither you nor your counsellor have failed — the counselling itself has simply not given you enough resources. Counselling is still a very inexact science and perfect results are rare.

It could also be that your return to counselling has nothing whatever to do with your previous issues. 'I'd go back into counselling tomorrow if I started to feel bad again, for whatever reason,' said Tamara. Many people, particularly if they are addressing more general problems, or doing generative work, slip in and out of counselling throughout their lives. Many counsellors will support you to take a break, often for integration purposes, and then come back; this is more usual in the private sector than in the NHS where resources have to be channelled onto immediate and acute problems.

Resuming and changing

'Stopping' may in fact be just a change of system, setting up a new form of counselling, often on the advice of your previous counsellor. There may be a gap of a few days, months or years, but the significant thing is that you resume counselling in a new way.

- You may change from individual to group counselling, or vice versa.
- You may move to or from a residential situation.
- You may move counsellors within the same clinic or organization.
- You may change approaches altogether.

Whatever happens, return to your original list of outcomes, as given in the check-list in Chapter 2, and rethink them. They will almost certainly be different now because you are a different person with a new set of experiences. Negotiate again to get your needs met.

You may be changing methods or counsellors because you feel disillusioned with your previous experience. If so, be wary of doing exactly the same thing again. Check very carefully that your outcomes are being met at the start, and if you find yourself nevertheless becoming unhappy with what is happening, think back over your life. Do you, like Dick did, have a 'pattern of resenting authority figures — I'd regularly blow out doctors and dentists, so I knew I had to be careful not to do the same with counsellors!' If you have a similar history, stick with your current counsellor for a while, discuss the pattern and use it as a focus for your personal work.

The Growth movement

Many of the clients we spoke to had gone on from their first experience in counselling to a more in-depth involvement in a variety of counselling-type activities. These were usually the people who had been drawn to counselling in the first place by a general need — for fulfilment, for spiritual development, for increased happiness — rather than by a specific crisis or issue, such as wanting to stop smoking.

These interviewees are representative of an entire sub-culture of people fascinated by, and active in their personal development, or 'growth' as it is more usually known. The growth movement is based around humanistic psychology[1], and comprises an informal network of individuals and organizations offering a bewildering variety of courses, groups and individual sessions. We see the difference as one of attitude — once you start identifying yourself as someone who is concerned with your personal change outside of just one particular issue or emotion, then you have effectively become part of the Growth movement.

People we spoke to said their longer-term involvement took a variety of forms. Usually, they combined one-to-one, group work and workshops with reading about a particular approach. Often they moved from one approach to another, with some overlap or with a short break in between. They sometimes took further training in particular approaches, often ending up leading workshops or integrating the skills they learned into their work.

We both came into counselling through the growth culture. As well as benefiting massively from the access it has given us to many different forms of counselling, we also recog-

[1] See Chapter 15.

nize its wider potential to achieve large-scale *social* change. We asked a number of our interviewees their reasons for devoting so much of their time and energy to such wide-ranging personal development. Here are some of the reasons they gave:

- It provides an ongoing support system to help them cope with day-to-day problems and occasional crises.
- It makes them more effective in their professional and personal lives.
- Workshops and group work give an emotional 'high' which makes it all worthwhile.
- It is their equivalent of going to an amateur dramatics group — they can act creatively and do things they wouldn't normally do.
- It is their equivalent of an evening class such as squash or embroidery — an enjoyable hobby.
- Groups and workshops offer an easily accessible social life with compatible and emotionally aware people.
- It gives a spiritual dimension to life which is not religion-based.
- It is a context in which to build their own, made-to-measure, personal development programme.
- It is their way of being good to themselves.

Ultimately, long-term, in-depth involvement with 'growth work' can range far beyond the counselling-based options we have mentioned in this book. It can span the more esoteric options, such as crystal healing or feminist ritual; more body-work options such as Rolfing or Feldenkreis; more business-based options such as stress management or personal coaching; more health options such as Alexander technique and Bach flower remedies. We even heard (though admittedly in California) of a visiting business acupuncturist who specializes in working with international banks! Once you begin, the sky's the limit! We list here some of the more obvious and enjoyable manifestations of the Growth movement in Britain today.

Books

Sections of most bookshops, and the entire stock of some 'alternative' bookshops[2] are devoted to personal change issues. Look under *Psychology, Personal development* or in high street branches, under *Health*. Our bibliography lists some starter books which will take you into more depth on the issues we talk about, and any of the associations listed in Chapters 14 and 15 will be happy to recommend their particular 'bibles' to you.

Magazines

Magazines on related subjects can be found in bookshops, growth and health centres, and health food shops. Most of the issue- and school-based organizations produce their own newsletters — the more general ones are listed in our bibliography. They provide up-to-date coverage of what is happening in terms of ideas, people and events in their particular area and are wonderful sources of information and inspiration — as well as counsellors and workshops.

Events

Large-scale exhibitions, like the annual Festival of Mind, Body and Spirit in London, provide forums for many national organizations and even individuals with something particular to offer. Local exhibitions, maybe held at your local holistic health centre, give the district co-counselling community a chance to advertise. Both kinds of exhibition can be enormous fun, a chance to talk to people and a chance to try things out. Beware, though, of exhibitors at what can be said to be the 'loony fringe' of the growth movement — the people who claim to have found the secret of everlasting life, or the salesmen with the magic potions. However, even these can be good entertainment!

Workshops

The workshop is perhaps the classic growth activity. A group of people come together for a day, a weekend or longer, to be guided by a skilled facilitator through some form of

---

[2] Bookshops with postal services that we have found to be reliable are also listed in the bibliography.

experience designed to facilitate awareness or development.

Workshops vary tremendously. While there are no hard and fast rules about what they will comprise, they usually include paired and group exercises involving talking, listening, dancing, acting or playing. There can be between six and sixty participants. At best, the experience is euphoric. If you are lucky enough for your workshop to be well run, and involve a good group of people, you will probably stay high for a week afterwards.

Many clients we talked to had moved from one-to-one counselling to workshops in their chosen approach, and many now ran the two activities in parallel. These were some of the comments made: 'They help me...understand the reasons behind what I'm doing in my sessions'. 'They give me a place to check my progress.' 'I love the games and fun we get in a group.' 'Sometimes what happens in the group stirs up something for me that I can work on back in my weekly counselling session.' 'Having other people around made the experience more powerful for me.'

Many of the approaches we have mentioned run group workshops in parallel with one-to-one or group counselling work. They are a good way of expanding your knowledge of the approach and speeding up your personal development. You don't have to be in one-to-one counselling before you can go to a workshop — many people get their first experience of personal change techniques in workshops. As we mentioned in Chapter 10, attending workshops is an excellent way to find a counsellor, especially if you live in a city such as Bristol, London, Sheffield, Brighton or York, which all have large growth communities.

If you are actually counselling at the time, you should check with your counsellor that going to workshops will not interfere with the work you are doing together. However for many clients, doing so is the natural next step, and will be totally supported by their counsellor.

Peer Groups

Peer-run groups can develop from any organization or approach when the clients themselves run the sessions or workshops. These are often found in the less hierarchical schools of counselling, such as Co-Counselling, where, once everyone has done the training and knows the rules, it is possible to pool resources and 'do it yourself'. You will know soon enough, from the ethos of whatever you are interested in, whether this is an option. Peer groups can combine the best bits of workshops — everyone suggests activities, leads games or facilitates exercises. However they can also degenerate into what has been termed 'messy democracy' where most of the time is spent arguing. 'Our peer group (on women's health issues) started beautifully, but after a while people lost energy for it. In the end, after only two people turned up for two consecutive weeks, we called it a day.'

Remember that if you have an issue which you feel deeply about, you can always start a peer group yourself. After all, every counselling organization existing was started by someone just like you, and many of them began as meetings of ordinary people who just wanted to help. Alcoholics Anonymous, for example, is a peer organization. If you do decide to go it alone, we recommend you read the excellent *In Our Own Hands* by Sheila Ernst and Lucy Goodison, which deals with feminist approaches but is relevant to anyone beginning a peer group, and *Co-operative and Community Group Dynamics* by Rosemary Randall and John Southgate, which deals with how to cope with the problems peer groups often create. Details of both of these are given in the Bibliography.

Getting involved in the organization

Another extension of your involvement in counselling, which can be totally separate from the 'workshop circuit', may be to get involved on a helping level in one of the counselling organizations you have encountered. We will be talking in the next chapter about doing this by becoming a counsellor yourself but there are other ways you can be involved.

Perhaps the organization you work for needs voluntary helpers, to answer the phones, stuff envelopes, make coffee. Maybe you have more specialist skills, such as decorating or accounting that you can offer. Fund-raising of all kinds may also be vital, and many people get involved in this way.

As you begin to find yourself drawn towards further involvement, it is important to be aware of your agendas — just as aware of them as when you were entering counselling. There are several possible agendas you might have:

- *To return some of the help you have been given.* Great — but check that your willingness to help is not fuelled only by guilt.

- *To continue the contact with the organization in order to get mutual support.* No-one will object to this, but check that it is realistic — once you are no longer in a counselling relationship, you will not get the same contract.

- *To make friends and develop your social life.* Some organizations encourage socializing among their helpers, but be warned, others hold that if your prime aim in working for them is to make friends, you may not give of your best.. Counselling organizations are traditionally wary of friendship anyway.[3]

- *To feel you are being useful.* You may be surprised to know that this motivation rings alarm bells for many counselling organizations. If you strongly need to feel you are useful (or likeable, etc.) in order to function, then you may hit problems and get disillusioned if the organization doesn't give you its approval all the time.

- *To prepare for a career move.* It is possible, as we explain in Chapter 11, to make a career of counselling, and this is a good way both to pick up good practice from those counsellors around you, and to explore whether you would like to do this sort of work all the time. But don't expect to get a job from it; experience with counselling organizations is useful when applying for a job in counselling, but jobs are so scarce that there are no guarantees of anything.

Longer-term views

In order to really answer the question 'What next?' you will need to look at your longer-term plans. This exploration helps you to focus in on what you really want to do — and perhaps what you want counselling to do for you — in a life context.

[3] See Chapter 7 on the problems of socializing with your counsellor.

Read through the questions below. You don't have to answer them right away; take your time, perhaps even a day or two to mull them over, talk them through with those close to you. Then, put your answers into action.

What sort of life do you want? What would you like to have done by the time you reach the last years of your life? In broad and realistic terms, what achievements, what relationships, what environments would you like to have created for yourself?

What sort of person will you need to be by the end of your life in order to do these things?

How is that person different from the way you are now?

What changes do you need to make, throughout your life?

How can you use counselling or the Growth movement in order to help you make those changes?

What resources do you need to gather in order to get that help (time, energy, determination, money, contacts etc)?

What is the first thing you need to do, right now, in order to start that happening?

Guy began growth work nine years ago by doing a short Co-Counselling course because of problems in his marriage. He enjoyed the counselling and found it gave him both a chance to work on himself and practice in listening skills. He attended workshops and residential weekends, and after a while began co-leading workshops himself. He then took two weekends and two ten-week evening courses of Gestalt, which he found useful and complementary to Co-Counselling. He thought of doing training to become a Gestalt therapist but instead, he did an eight-weekend NLP course, with weekly practice sessions. He followed this by beginning a hypnotherapy course, but dropped out after the first weekend because he did not like the training style. While continuing to use the other disciplines he had learned, he then took a massage course and a reflexology course end-on over the course of eight months. He is currently doing a fortnightly training course in transpersonal psychology, having done seven weekend courses with the Transpersonal Centre. He is also teaching Co-Counselling and practises as an independent therapist, and stress management consultant, using both his bodywork and counselling skills.

Chapter 11

Becoming a counsellor

When you have received a great deal from counselling, a natural step is to want to return it — and a natural impulse is to want to be a counsellor yourself.

Helen began by receiving one-way counselling when she was recovering from a divorce. She then progressed to Co-Counselling, where she both received and gave help to work through problems. After a year of regular counselling, she moved on to work in an adolescent unit, as a part-time helper, whilst going on a day-release counselling course. 'I got involved because I needed help. When I realized what that could do, I wanted to give some of it back.'

How to use this chapter

This chapter covers the broad issues of *whether* and *how* to become a counsellor. It contains:

- A list of questions to answer which will help you to find out whether you are suitable to become a counsellor.

- A section on what you would be giving and what you would be getting by doing so.

- A review of some of the routes we found people taking to get there.

Whether to become a counsellor

First, consider whether you have the motivation to do so. For becoming a counsellor, as any training organization will tell you, is not just a matter of wanting to help other people. We have listed a number of questions that individual counsellors and counselling organizations have suggested that you ask yourself when you are deciding.

Have you already been in counselling?

If you've ever been tempted to think that having been in counselling somehow makes you not quite equal to those who are counselling you, consider this: the majority of professional counselling organizations will not accept you for training unless you are yourself engaged in a serious programme of being counselled. The reasons for this are many: unless you have been in counselling, you will be unable to really appreciate the client's viewpoint; if you are to be a counsellor, you will need to demonstrate a serious commitment to your own personal growth; you need to have standards of comparison and experiences of counselling for yourself; being a counsellor requires a *very* stable personality, and that needs working at.

The Westminster Pastoral Foundation[1], for example, request that in order to follow their programme, you do at least one session a week with a counsellor and probably more, for the entire course of two or more years. The requirement for counselling isn't usually as stringent as this for volunteer counsellor programmes which usually ask only that you undergo their training programme.

Are you committed to a particular issue or approach?

This is by no means essential in order to become a counsellor, but we did find that most of the counsellors and many of the trainees we spoke to were committed. Often it was to the very issue that they had had themselves when they

[1] WPF runs the largest programme of counselling training in the country. They run a variety of full and part-time courses, all lasting several years.

came into counselling, or the very approach that helped them most. People we spoke to found that it focused their work to have a specialism; it also helped them to find a market when they moved into professional work. For example, when Janet found she had a vocation for counselling, she used her art training as the emotional and practical basis for her work as an art therapist.

Can you support your counselling from your lifestyle?

This question covers both material and emotional support. Even after training, many forms of counselling are unpaid, or paid at a nominal fee, whilst part-time work, such as that often done for organizations like the Samaritans[2], takes up a few hours a week. If you wish to set up as a full-time private counsellor, it can often take a long time to build a practice. It is also very rare to get a counselling post that is salaried, particularly with the current financial situation in the NHS. If you do plan to take up counselling full time, you will need to treat it like any other free-lance career, and expect to make a loss at the beginning. However, running a private counselling practice at a loss in the long-term is destructive for both counsellors and clients — the counsellor gets resentful and loses self-esteem, and the clients get the message that the skills they are being offered are worthless. If you are working within an organization, though, there will often be enough group energy to sustain you as a volunteer — and in any case, you will probably be doing it in addition to your normal wage-earning activity.

You will also need to check that you are likely to receive sufficient emotional support for your counselling training and career. Some courses involve practical training of eight to ten hours, but the study for a full professional qualification can be long and arduous, involving a commitment of one to three days' a week class time plus extra study, supplementary counselling for yourself, and supervised counselling with others. Interviewees spoke to us of the very real strain of this plus the fact that, 'You never know if you are

---

[2] Samaritans don't like to be called counsellors but we think that they *are* counsellors, and their tiny 16-hour training course impresses us more than some that last years.

going to complete the course, as the standards are so high that not everyone passes.' Given sufficient practical and emotional support, being a counsellor can be a superbly rewarding experience, but you do need to have friends, partners or relatives there to help you. This is another reason why many counselling courses insist on you receiving support yourself during the course.

Do you have the qualifications?

The question of qualifications is a tricky one. There are many organizations using excellent counsellors with no qualifications at all, and many individual counsellors whose only qualification is that they are good at their job. However, some organizations, the NHS included, insist on quite high-level qualifications before they will let you loose on clients.

If you want to apply for a professional training course, which gives you formal counselling qualifications, it is likely you will already need to have some level of formal education, or a great deal of experience in the field or both. Requirements differ from course to course though, and the best thing to do is to apply direct to these courses through the institutes who run them to find out in detail if you will be acceptable. If you wish to train in some organizations, however, such as the Samaritans and many issue-based agencies, your primary need is to have the personal qualities and commitment necessary.

Are you only wanting to help?

We have refused participants on our Co-Counselling training courses because they said their overriding aim was to help other people. This can so often lead to 'rescuing' others, or being dragged down into their distress. A feeling that you only want to help is probably hiding some needs of your own. We put far more trust in a healthy degree of selfishness, a sentiment that we would expect most counselling trainers to echo.

What will you give and what will you get?

One key issue that came through in our conversations with counsellors and counselling agencies was that you need to know clearly why you want to be a counsellor. Take the time to make a list of what you think you will gain, and what you think you have to give. Only if the two balance and complement each other will you be happy in, and suitable for, the counselling profession, whether that is on a voluntary or professional, full or part-time basis. The following check-list might help you:

What will you gain from counselling?

Information
Support
Insight
Change
Other

Just as these attracted you to seek counselling, so they will underlie your wish to become a counsellor. One on its own will make you unbalanced as a professional, while a mixture of two or more will ensure a more professional approach. It is no good just offering clients information, while blocking their change process, nor is it helpful to insist that they have insights while failing to see the importance of supporting them emotionally while they work towards that. Decide for yourself which motivations are compelling you to become a counsellor — and be aware of what your gaps are.

What will you give to counselling?

Skills
Experience
Motivation
Time
Energy
Other

It is just as vital to be aware of what you have to offer. List your resources under each heading, being aware that a balance is better than (say) a great deal of experience, but no time. Remember that all of the above can be created —

counselling courses aim to give you the first two if you have the others, and if counselling is truly important to you, you will rearrange your life so that the time and energy are there.

From reading through the above notes, you will probably have begun to get a feeling for whether you *want* to be a counsellor, and whether you are *suitable*. If the answer to the first question is no, there is no longer an issue for you to consider. If the answer to the second question is no, we suggest you contact one of the counselling training organizations and discuss with them how you could go about changing yourself, your situation or your qualifications in order to become more suitable.

If the answer to both questions is yes, read on.

Sophie left university with a degree in psychology and a desire to help people. She worked for a year to earn the money to do a full-time counselling training, and then joined one of the major training organizations, to do a full-time course. At first, it was as interesting as her degree, but slowly she found that, 'There was too much Angst. I felt dragged down by all the emotion.' Her supervisor confirmed that Sophie was indeed not progressing as well as she could have, and Sophie left the course. She is now working as a personnel officer in a large department store, and still enjoys helping people — but 'on a much lighter level.'

How to become a professional counsellor

Whilst talking to our interviewees, we identified several routes to becoming a counsellor, which we outline briefly here. For further details contact the relevant addresses in Chapters 14 and 15.

'People just asked me for sessions'

Janet was a good listener, and one day got paid just for listening. 'A client had a stroke and I visited her in hospital; when she came home, she asked if I was taking clients, and something told me to say yes. She said, 'Right, book me in.'

A few of the counsellors we spoke to drifted into being professionals because they knew people who wanted counselling. If you are aware of personal growth issues, particularly if you have done workshops and one-to-one sessions yourself, you may well develop not only a number of contacts who are interested in counselling for themselves, but also the skills necessary to give them that. If you are given good counselling yourself, you often learn how to give it in return, almost by a process of osmosis, and on one level this works well. On another level though this is something to be wary of. Unless you have had some form of formal training, you may enter counselling unprotected, and unable to avoid getting sucked into other people's distress and give them the objective, loving help they deserve. It is wise, if you find yourself listening to friends, enjoying that, maybe being recommendeu to strangers, to look seriously at getting some back-up training in professional skills.

Co-Counselling

Co-Counselling, an approach we describe in more detail on page 111, can be seen as a half-way house between listening to friends and professional counselling. We have found that the training it offers is highly valued within the counselling community, and that the skills it develops are certainly sufficient to promote personal change in the clients you work with. Its reciprocal system also supplies one essential feature of any long-term counselling training, regular work on yourself. Co-Counselling is also aimed at introducing people to a network of counsellor/client possibilities, and so gives you the opportunity to do a lot of counselling, do a lot of clienting, and learn skills from other people. What it doesn't give is training in dealing with clients who are not trained in the same system as yourself. In Co-Counselling, unlike any other counselling situation, everyone knows how to be a client and take responsibility for themselves.

As a first step towards professional humanistic counselling training, we can unhesitatingly recommend a basic Co-Counselling course. It is the most accessible route into person-centred[3] counselling and opens the way for you to

[3] See Chapter 15.

practise both counselling and clienting until you are sure that this is a route you want to pursue. A full professional counselling training, of course, it is not.

Voluntary counselling

Another basic step in learning to counsel may be to join one of the counselling organizations as a voluntary counsellor. It helps if you have experience of the issue around which the organization is based, either for yourself or through someone near to you. Many successful help-lines have been started, and are now staffed, by people who came into counselling driven by a need to solve that particular problem. The Hysterectomy Support Group, for example, is made up of women who have all had hysterectomies themselves.

If you begin work as a voluntary counsellor, you will almost certainly be given a basic training course followed up by regular refresher courses. In addition, your work will be 'supervised', which means that you have someone to whom you can take any problems you cannot deal with, and to whom you can turn, if and when you become affected by the counselling you are giving. This structure is similar to that used in professional counselling training, but the training is not usually so intensive.

One disadvantage of voluntary counselling is obviously that if your first priority is to make a living from your work, this is not possible. However, as a way into counselling, a way of receiving good basic training, a way of finding out if the work suits you, and a way of giving back freely what you have received, it is excellent.

Professional training

Professional counselling training divides once again into many different types. You can get training to supplement a job you are already doing, especially if it is in a caring profession such as teaching or nursing, although we have not covered this kind of professional help in this book.

You can also do a basic counselling course at an evening class, which will usually be designed to introduce you to a range of possibilities so that you can then decide where to go from there. 'The *Introduction to Counselling* course I went on,' said Lorna, 'covered six different kinds of counselling over an eight-week course. By the end, we all knew what was what, and those who weren't convinced simply faded away.'

You can do a series of short, evening or weekend courses in a variety of disciplines, such as the ones we have mentioned in Chapter 15, and end up with an eclectic approach to counselling, moving from there to take private clients. As we mentioned earlier, the lack of a 'recognized' qualification means that you are likely to find yourself debarred from calling yourself a counsellor and working with certain kinds of clients in the future, such as those referred by private medical insurance. However, we believe there will still be people who have come up through the eclectic route who see clients and do good work, whatever they call themselves.

Finally, you can go to one of the major counselling training organizations, and do a full course which will take you all the way to a professional qualification. This may be full time or part time, and take several years of hard work, but at the end you will be able to apply for one of the jobs in the state system, or set up on your own as a private counsellor.

Patrick worked as a social worker for five years, but eventually became disillusioned. 'Firstly, I was overburdened with admin., so I had too little time to really talk to people, and secondly I stopped believing that I was actually helping the people I was supposedly there to serve.' Eventually, he left the social services and took a part-time job so that he could go to counselling classes two days a week. After the first year of classes, he started to see his own clients. Since then, he has slowly built up a practice as a private counsellor, specializing in family problems. 'It's a lot less lucrative than social work and often more hassle, but, when all's said and done, I find it intensely satisfying.'

Final thoughts

This chapter only scratches the surface of the process of becoming a counsellor. We have only tried to point you in the right direction. If you have decided that this is for you, however, you will get there whatever route you choose, and however long it takes.

If you want to be a counsellor, you will be.

Section 2

The experience

Chapter 12
Talking to clients

No consumer guide would be complete without consumer reports. In this chapter we recount a variety of accounts from people who have been through a number of counselling experiences, some good, some bad. We would add that we feel, as do our interviewees, that counselling experiences vary so much from counsellor to counsellor and client to client that these reports are not definitive, and that where a criticism is made it is not about an approach or a style as such, but only about that particular pairing of counsellor and client. That said, we hope you will gain from this chapter:

- An insight into the general experience of being a client
- Further guidelines as to what motivates people to enter counselling, and how they choose their counsellor and counselling approach
- Further knowledge of what is involved in particular kinds of counselling
- Models of how to deal with at least some of the many issues and problems that come up in counselling
- Inspiration to make the most of your counselling.

We have, where possible, used our interviewees' actual words, although we have edited text to avoid repetition and clarify unclear points. All the changes and the final text you see here have been approved by the interviewees themselves.

Rosamund — emergency counselling

Rosamund is in her mid-thirties and has a long-standing relationship. Her story illustrates a well-known kind of emergency counselling which meets a very specific need at a particular time.

I'd actually thought of ringing the Samaritans a few times before, but never quite got to do it. Once, I actually picked up the phone and dialled the number but it was engaged.

My boyfriend and I were going through a fairly bad time and we'd just had a big row and he'd walked out. This was last summer. I was in the flat on my own and there was this big sort of rock of feeling inside me that just totally overwhelmed me. I kept rushing round throwing things on the floor and tearing things up, just talking to myself; well, shouting most of the time. I thought I must be going mad.

I'm not sure whether I thought of killing myself. I did get to the drawer with the aspirin, but I kept thinking of having to have my stomach pumped, and of another time when I'd actually taken an overdose and ended up in Outpatients. All I felt then was embarrassed. I was frightened of dying, anyway. I don't actually want to be dead, but I did need it to stop — what I was feeling.

I thought of phoning up friends, but I thought I'd pour it all out and then just feel really ashamed, and I couldn't bear them to know we were having such a big row. So I kept going to the phone and dialling someone's number and then putting the phone down and crying again. I was in a total state.

I think I rang the Samaritans because I knew I'd be anonymous. I just wanted to cry and talk about it but with no questions asked — just someone to listen. When I dialled, I almost hoped they wouldn't answer, but a girl did. As soon as I heard her voice I started crying again, and just went on and on for ages.

After, a bit I started talking again, and she listened. It was exactly what I needed in some ways, though in other ways I wished she'd have *asked* more. I felt a bit as if I was the one doing all the feeling and she was at the other end of the phone being all cool. But I absolutely didn't need advice.

She asked my name, and gave me hers, and that felt odd, even though I knew that I'd never meet her. I told her about the row and about my boyfriend walking out, and then as far as I can remember she asked other things about our relationship. I think she was trying to get some sort of picture — probably whether or not there had been violence, or whether we had kids or something. I remember her asking me if I had 'thought of doing anything silly' and I thought, 'Oh here we go, she wants to know how close I am to taking the pills.' There was something about that that was funny, I thought (but I don't think she thought this) that if I said no, she'd lose interest and just think I was hysterical. I said I wasn't sure, but not really, which I think was the truth.

She did try to get me to talk it through, and said some things about how I could think about it in a different way, but I think really that what I needed was just someone to listen. I started getting embarrassed once I'd cried all I needed to. In some ways, because of that, I cut off from her once I felt better. In the end, I just wanted to get off the phone and have time to myself to think. I couldn't work out how to finish the conversation — I felt sort of grateful to her, but as if I wanted to be on my own.

Afterwards, I felt really good about ringing the Samaritans, although it didn't actually solve any problems. I know that even if I hadn't actually talked to someone, I would have survived, but at the time I kept feeling that I'd burst if I didn't have someone there, now, this minute, to give me some attention and actually to make me feel like a human being again. I would ring them again if I got desperate, although I might just warn them that I don't need to talk about my problems, I just need to cry and then put the phone down. But I don't know, maybe I'd need something different next time.

Sam — looking for emotional sharing

Sam tells of taking up and then moving on from a number of counselling styles. He shows how we can use counselling to meet our needs as they arise, and to continue to meet them even though these needs change.

It all started in 1980 when I came back from Egypt, and basically gave up the job I was doing. I decided I didn't want to do the job which I had always dreamed of doing and which I'd given up a relationship for and left the country for.

When I came back, I had nothing and I also had to answer fairly deep questions about the things I was getting value out of. At the time, people seemed to have very cut and dried views about what they wanted out of life, like status, money, a good job. I was finding that what I needed was much more about people and personal contacts, and this was what I needed in order to make the decisions I really needed to make.

I think I went into counselling in order to find a community of people who spoke the same language as me, who had been through the same experiences as me and could share them. The feeling was that people didn't talk about the emotional turmoil I was going through — they saw it as a sign of weakness. I wanted to meet people who were going through similar emotions and could talk about them, deal with them. I was looking for support, not advice. I was looking for insight through meeting others who were going through the same thing. It was fortuitous really that I got a flat in Putney which I was sharing with a friend and he had done EST training, and was quite into humanistic psychology.

My first experience, was, in fact, with somebody from a large central London practice, who I found very psychoanalytic. I think it's just a question of what you come across — I came across this advert for this person. I went along for three or four sessions, stared at a wall with a painting on it, talked almost the whole time with very little feedback and felt that I just wasn't getting anywhere. This wasn't the right thing for me, so I basically said that I was discontinuing.

Then, because I knew someone who'd done the EST training and who told me how helpful that had been to them I did that. I sort of reacted against the psychoanalytical thing. I did the EST training which, at the time, I found very valuable and moved me on a lot and got me out of my depression. But as I got more involved in the EST organization and started working at their offices on a voluntary basis for a short time, I got quite turned off about what they were doing and the way they were organized.

Then, I'm not quite sure how, I got involved in Co-Coun-selling. I saw an advert I think, and thought that I liked the peer group principle, and I liked the fact that you're train-ing as a counsellor *and* you're helping other people too. This, too, had a group element to it. Perhaps there was a learn-ing curve; I was moving on, rejecting what I didn't like and finding more and more what I did like — from psychoanal-ysis through EST to Co-Counselling. I reacted against the authoritarianism and intellectualism of EST by going to the eclecticism and peer principles of Co-Counselling. It fulfilled quite a few criteria going into Co-Counselling at that time.

I did the Co-Counselling Fundamentals course and then counselled with people for about six months. I met a cou-ple of very good friends through Co-Counselling with them, and I found there was a danger of slipping into friendships with counsellors rather than keeping a counselling relation-ship, so the whole thing began to flounder. Also I found difficulty with deep discharge. So I stopped doing Co-Counselling and, in a way, left self-development for about three years. But I went through a number of experiences — I did a lot of work with a friend who was a massage ther-apist which helped me to open up and trust.

Then I went to a Co-Counselling workshop in Sheffield that a friend was running and got back into it again. There was a lot of body work in that workshop and it opened the floodgates for discharge. Instead of having to be rational about it all and coming from my head, I was coming from my body and discharge was suddenly nothing of a problem. So it kind of burst things open for me and I got back into Co-Counselling.

From this point I had a long-term Co-Counselling rela-tionship for three years with the same person. We'd coun-sel with each other once a week or once a fortnight and I found it extremely useful. But eventually the fact that we weren't counselling at all outside our sessions made them, I think, quite a narrow and prescribed. Despite the fact that we would reflect every few months and ask in what ways we were colluding with each other, I still think that unless you have outside experiences, just counselling with one other person can become narrowing after a while. And that is what happened; the repertoire of what we were doing became restricted even though we were drawing on Gestalt and bodywork, and even though I would go to the occasional workshop. However, I must say I found it very beneficial, the intimacy of being able to share with another person. If one isn't in an intimate relationship, I think it's important to have that, to have a space where you can share things and be creative, go with wild ideas, practise things like interviews before going through them.

That relationship basically finished only a few months ago, by mutual consent. Towards the end of it, I had been dabbling in other things like NLP, and had even been teaching some self-development things at the college where I work.

At the moment, I've plunged straight into Psychosynthesis. I've done something which I've never done before, which is abandoned myself to the process rather than being intellectual about it. I've spoken to several people I respect who have found Psychosynthesis very valuable, and for me what was important was that it was very much about self-expression and it had a very strong spiritual element. Both of these are very important for me at this point.

Today, in fact, I've been reflecting back on the sessions I've had. So far I've only had five sessions and they've been extraordinarily useful and powerful. These are one-to-one sessions with a counsellor, totally one way. In my work, I have been very intellectual, and I've been very much up in my head. Doing Psychosynthesis, I'm coming from a totally different place. A lot of it is non-verbal, a lot of it is a meditative state, allowing feelings to come up and be there. I don't need to overtly express them, I don't need to pound cushions, but I still feel the feelings. I've found it very dynamic and deep — on one occasion I got into an ecstatic state, which is something I haven't experienced for some time.

It's a very gentle process, and I have a good sense about the therapist I'm working with. She had a lot of integrity about checking things out when we work, and there is space for me to say, 'No, I don't want to do this.' It's also very much linked to my everyday life; we've been doing work on how I can take things back to my life. It's made me look at what I am doing every day, stop and reflect, give myself space to behave differently, give myself time to notice what's going on for me.

The benefits I've had since starting counselling work on myself are so many that I'd find it difficult to give a complete list; skills for my career, life planning, more creativity, insight about other people and more tolerance for them, more experience of feelings which I can't remember experiencing before.

Issues I've worked on? I've done a lot about my relationships with women, work and overwork, self-expression. I've done a lot of work on coming to terms with my feelings about my father and getting to relate to him. Counselling helped a lot, both while my father was still alive and now he's dead. It was important to me that before he died I was able to form a relationship with him that was expressive and loving. For that alone, being in counselling has been worth it.

I feel that really good quality counselling is like a tightrope walk. It can result in relying too much on the therapist; you begin to lose sight of the fact that it's about oneself and working oneself. Good old dependence! Also, the counsellor isn't always right. You really have to maintain an awareness about whether the counsellor is doing what's best for you, and be able to say that straight out. That isn't always easy; with certain forms of therapy you're just not encouraged to take on that role. I feel it's very important, but difficult because often by the nature of the trust you put into being with a counsellor, you might feel that you are stepping over a line.

I can think of quite a number of really excellent memories of counselling; there are a number that have been good for very different reasons. Recently in a Psychosynthesis session, I felt as if I was diving down through all the layers, and accepting everything inside me; I reached a state of real joy which was quite overwhelming.

Carlye — wanting someone to talk to her

Carlye entered counselling at a very specific time of her life to get guidance and support. She shows how counselling can be a part of your life for a short period, and then having done its job, cease. She also illustrates how you can search for a counsellor and eventually find one who suits you.

My ex-husband left me and wouldn't say that he wanted a divorce. He seemed to be making coming back conditional on my going to a therapist. I only realized afterwards that he was afraid that I was going to kill myself, and wanted me to get support, which was quite considerate. I didn't really know what I was looking for in counselling. So I went to the first therapist, who was not at all good. My husband's therapist recommended her. I went to one visit and she drew me a little chart with words like 'individuation' and 'separation' on a white board, and I felt this wasn't right for me, and it wasn't what I needed. That was one session and then I said, 'Forget it'.

A couple of months after that I went to Virginia, whom I found through a friend. By that time my agenda was really different; I was very self-destructive in feeling, and I knew I really needed something. I knew by then that Tom wasn't coming back.

I stayed with Virginia for about nine months. She tried to get me to commit for two to three years, but the problem with her was that she was quite expensive and she had a habit of standing me up on sessions. I didn't like her — she wasn't in or of herself very much use to me as a therapist. I think the fact I got so much out of the sessions is a tribute to me.

When I finished school, I moved to a different city and so I stopped my counselling. I didn't want to, but I knew that Virginia wasn't that much good anyway. Then I went to a third therapist, because my boss was driving me crazy. I liked my boss a lot, but she was extremely demanding — just like a lot of female figures in my life. I realized I shouldn't just go and get a different better job, I should try to deal with it.

So I went to this therapist who was really horrible; I always insisted on having a woman because I knew I wouldn't be able to handle counselling with a man. I remember her well, she put me off right away because she was coated with make-up and had long red nails. She did lots of really terrible things — first she asked me very personal questions in a really voyeuristic way, then she kept me waiting ten minutes, had me leave ten minutes early and asked me to leave the office while she took a personal phone call.

Then I found Ruth. I was looking for someone who could

and would respond to me intelligently. My accountant said that his girl friend had a really good therapist that she really liked. When I called her on the phone and she said, 'What are you looking for?' I said, 'I'm looking for someone who will talk to me.' She was great and I stayed with her for about eight months, and she charged a reasonable amount of money. Money is always an issue in counselling, for the counsellor as well as the client.

I also realize that with Ruth I was looking for a mother, whatever that means. Probably I didn't realize that until after I'd left therapy. I needed someone to help me internalize several things — self-esteem, optimism, ability to deal with failure, things I think every human needs in order to help them through life. That was something I didn't get from my mother, but I did get them from Ruth. I still feel towards her the way I would feel towards a really good mother. For example, I didn't have a lot of separation anxiety about leaving, in fact, that was what made me realize that she had been a 'good mother' — it wasn't that bad to leave.

Throughout all the counselling I was working on relationships — the relationship with my boss, which echoed the relationships I've had with a lot of women in my life in intensity and structure. My relationships with men, particularly my husband. Relationships... relationships with women and relationships with men, and, of course, my relationship with myself.

With Ruth, we did an awful lot of, 'How do I deal with this?' With her help, I'd work out quite specific advice on what attitudes to have, and how to deal with things in a very practical, positive way. Then I'd go out and try it. That was what I found most helpful. We didn't actually do a lot of digging into childhood. I guess she was a behaviourist — knowing what was wrong wasn't important, but finding a way to deal with what was wrong *was* important. I don't really remember things not working out when I went out and tried them — but success or failure wasn't important. When things didn't work out, we thought about how to forgive yourself.

I think so much of what happens in counselling between counselling and client is a matter of fit. I think a lot of people get screwed by the academic 'silence', which I don't like, which didn't work for me. My particular problem was that

I felt that people didn't respond to me. So to go in and say to a counsellor, 'People don't respond to me' and for them to say nothing is awful. Other people may want something less intrusive.

Also, another thing for me is that many therapists have this thing that they won't confirm anything for you because you ought to learn to rely on your own self-esteem and not rely on them for confirmation. But if you've never learned to confirm anything for yourself, that's very difficult to deal with. What is needed is someone who you trust and respect and who is an authority figure to teach you how to confirm for yourself what you are thinking and feeling, so you aren't feeling, 'Is it me? or Is it them?' I remember Ruth saying to me that something my boss was doing was totally off the wall, and it was such a relief to be told it wasn't me and it wasn't my problem. After 26 years of wondering whether it was me that was odd, it was so good to realize that I was OK.

Janet — from receiving to giving

Janet began as a client moving through a number of counselling methods including some bodywork styles. Now she has reached a point where she knows she wants to help others by being a counsellor herself.

I was into a high-powered public relations job. I was being swallowed up by pressure because I didn't realize at the time that the more you do, the more they push on to you, until your health says, 'If you don't do something about it, I will.' That's what happened. My voice gave out. I just couldn't talk.

My doctor had already suggested I see someone to get support. She put it very nicely; she asked me who talked to my children when they had a problem. So I said that generally they come and talk to me. 'Who talks to your ex-husband, or your in-laws when they have problems.' 'They come to me.' And she said, 'So, who do you go to?' I agreed to give it a whirl, and went to see the head psychiatric nurse and after half an hour she said to me, 'I think you should be in my chair. I think I'd like to tell you some of my problems. . .' It was nice to talk to her because it boosted my morale, but. . .

In the end, I left. My voice kept cutting out and they weren't going to put up with that for long. One night I was sitting here with my sons when one of them said to the other — as if it was another planet almost — 'There's no point in asking her anything. She doesn't come round until about ten o'clock.' And something clicked. That night I sat down and wrote out my resignation.

What then? My friend needed her house doing up and said she would pay me £100 a week to do it. I did that and some French polishing and then my friend said, 'Will you do the garden for me?' and that's how the gardening started.

I found that, through the gardening, I seemed to get involved not just with the gardens but a lot with people's lives. It seemed to me especially with a lot of the elderly people that I got the reception 'Oh it's lovely to see you, Jan. Now I've got someone to talk to.' I was sitting down listening to all their problems and saying, consciously or unconsciously, 'Wouldn't it be better if you. . .' and then someone said to me, 'Oh Jan, you always seem to be able to turn the negative into the positive.' So then I thought, 'How can I help people more and how can I help myself?'

I realized that through the gardening, my body was screaming left right and centre. I had already started doing yoga; it began very much as a purely physical thing, but then I became much more aware of how my body and mind were working. My yoga teacher came up and told me that I had a tremendous amount of healing power around me, and that interested me. I also remember, a good eight or ten years ago now, that on a yoga workshop the teacher spoke about the tree of life. I visualized the tree of life very clearly and saw myself going up different branches and going off into twigs. That's how I view life now, with the end result as the top of the tree, but always trying something new. But then, Yoga seemed not to be enough, so I went to have an intuitive massage once a week. I did this for about nine months on and off.

I felt I wanted to get more involved in intuitive things such as massage and aromatherapy, but also I thought that counselling is quite a strong number and that I'd like to be able to use it more positively in the work that I'm doing. The massage lady said I should go and see a person she had heard about, so I rang Sue up and said, 'What I'd really like to do is to have a chat to you to see if you could help me sort out what would be right for me to do.' I had an hour's consultation with Sue to do with the job, and she suggested lots of things I could do. As a result of having that hour, I spontaneously said to her, 'Have you got another hour, an hour's counselling?' I worked with Sue for a while, and, at the end, she said, 'Gosh, you've moved very fast. I feel you could go and do Co-Counselling now.'

So I did a Co-Counselling Fundamentals course. I found it was helpful, but I also feel life is about the here and now, not the past. After the fundamentals, a group of about six of us formed our own little peer group. I agreed to do a session on body work for the group. A lot of things came up from that. I found it very stimulating and enjoyed doing it. I was nervous beforehand, but afterwards pleased that I'd done it. Now I'm dropping out. I feel a little bit as if the group isn't really advanced enough for me.

I'm also at present doing some NLP, because the lady I do Yoga with said, 'I really think this is a course you could get a lot out of.' I also have therapy every Monday afternoon with another therapist. I've also done many other things. I started going to a spiritual centre which did colour healing and I've done the ITEC massage course. Everything I do I gain something from, nothing has ever been a total waste of time or money. I think I'm spending money on my education, which I really feel I didn't have as a child. I value myself enough that I want to spend that money.

I realize that I've got a lot of work to do on myself, but that's exciting. I always find it exciting. Even when I get low and feel everything is getting on top of me, I always know at the back of my mind that I'll come out and it will all be new and exciting.

I'm looking to start working with clients soon. I got talking to a doctor whose garden I did. I recognized that when I arrived one day, although he said he was fine, he wasn't. He talked to me about his problems and later rang me up and said it had helped, and could he give me something. I said he could give me a donation, and I was staggered when he put £25 in my hand. Then another gardening client had a stroke and I visited her in hospital. When she came home, she asked me if I was doing massage yet. Something told me to say yes, and she said, 'Right, book me in.'

So this year, because I decided I wanted to move into taking counselling clients, I cut my gardening clients by half, and have decided to see what happens. This is my year of learning, and I'm learning a lot. If anyone reads this and says, 'Well, I can't afford to do that', I would say to them I left my job with £1,000 in the bank, and there have been times when it's been tough, but I see that as being positive.

Tamara — dealing with a specific problem

Tamara is in her late twenties. She was forced to give up a promising career in theatre stage management through injury. The sudden loss of her job forced her to look at many other uncertainties in her life.

I've only had two journeys into counselling in my life.

First of all, I had been recommended to a Biodynamic centre. Their approach was very much using a stethoscope and massaging, and we didn't actually get as far as talking about my problems. After three sessions, I realized that this wasn't actually right for me; not that I necessarily wanted results immediately, but when I asked them why they were still massaging me, and I was ready to talk, they said they didn't think they could approach my mind while my body was in such a state. I have this back injury, which catapulted me into going into counselling, made me reassess my life. My feeling was that my back isn't going to get better, but if my mind gets better, that will help it. I could have carried on being massaged for months, but I felt the problem was in my head and if that was put right my body would follow suit.

I quickly realized that I was in a buyer's market, and that what I was doing was wrong for me. I rang them up and told them and said that I didn't think that it was the type of therapy I was looking for. They were fine with that. Then I was recommended to Ian by my flatmate Jan, and she was saying, 'You'll be fine with him. I know he's a man and you feel you don't want to work with men, but he's really an honorary woman!' As far as I'm concerned, therapy can only come through recommendation of people you trust, respect and love. A number of my friends have been in therapy and they will not talk about their therapy, but I like to tell people about my counselling — I think people deserve what I got, just to help them feel better.

I was with him for about eight sessions, basic therapy for about an hour and a lot of talking after that, though I always thought about things a lot between sessions. I was extremely daunted by the entire prospect, but at the first session, I was feeling very good, and so when I actually got myself to go to him and he sat me down and said, 'What's wrong?' I actually had to sit and think, 'Well, what is wrong?', I've known what I wanted for years and years, but I hadn't found a way through to getting it.

It was fantastic — exactly the right approach. It keyed in to what I needed completely and sorted out so many things. I've considered that the things below the surface needed changing, but I hadn't been able to break the boundaries of my own thought. I needed someone to throw the focus on things for me. The kind of counselling that Ian was helping me with made me view myself in a different way and exorcize a lot of ghosts.

It was very easy to talk to him. It wasn't necessarily always probing questions and I didn't feel put on the spot, or that I needed to perform. We did a lot of role play, and going into other people I know and viewing me or a situation from another standpoint. I found it incredibly difficult to do, but it had never occurred to me before, and I have found it very useful both during the counselling and since. I use it, of course, in my work — I've gone on to do a theatre director's course now. I've always had a good veneer, but the outside and the inside never quite tallied. The counselling has helped me to put the two together.

I've had problems in my life, and I've always related that back to the fact that my father left when I was six or seven years old. I've always resented him horribly for that and he's always had huge power over me. Even though he was over the other side of the world, he has always had economic or emotional power. I always thought that my problems were related back to that. I also have always had this big gap in my head, pre-six or seven and post-six or seven, around the time that my Dad left. I really couldn't remember anything before that; I just wanted to shut down the memory banks on all that.

I get this knot in my sternum when things go wrong or I'm hiding things, or when I can't say, 'I love you' or 'I don't like you.' Ian asked me to relate that feeling back to experiences, and I found it very difficult to get right back, so I had to relate it through photos and stories told to me. I managed to do that, and I went back into actually giving my father a personality — for, as Ian pointed out, he was a symbol rather than a person. What I did was to go back to different situations when he was there or when he wasn't there and I wanted him to be there, and work out a personality for him, demystify him. His power's gone now, I don't resent him any more. I went back to being the little girl looking up and then the adult looking down and I realized that the adult looking down is one of my contemporaries. He was only a few years older than I am now when he left us — which is mind-boggling.

The major thing I realized was that the dichotomy between my outer self and my inner self actually stems from my mother, who I love very deeply and get on well with. I realized that it was in relation to her concerning my father that I had started to hide things, not show that I was upset and be happy-go-lucky on the surface because I didn't want her to feel guilty about my emotions and make life more difficult for her. Suddenly there was this weird different underplay which was like getting a thunderbolt between the eyes. Having put myself into her thoughts and feelings in the counselling, I don't resent her. She was doing exactly what she felt was right; it was her way of coping with her emotions. It was putting an awful lot of responsibility onto a six, seven, eight, ten, fifteen year old — me. Now that I understand it, I don't blame her, and I cannot be upset by it. I can now be completely honest with her. That was the really major thing that happened to me in counselling.

I'm bursting with how it's changed my life. It's made me a lot less frightened of failure because I actually don't think I'm going to. I'm a lot less guilty about saying things, demanding things, and I'm a lot more open about emotions. Soon after I started counselling a relationship I was having split up. Normally I would have taken responsibility for this and think that it was me that failed, but instead I went into the break up and demanded to know certain facts and certain things. I said, 'I love you, I still want you, the door is open', which I wouldn't have said before. I would have been so concerned with the rejection. I came out feeling like death, but uncompromised and with my belief in myself much stronger than before. Even though I was mourning for the end of a relationship, I came out feeling so much better about myself. Ian said to me in the therapy, 'You can do so much talking in the little room with the chairs, but then you have to put it into action.' I feel that I did.

A lot of my friends are in therapy and have been for two or three years. It seems as if they are using it as an emotional crutch, but I don't want or feel I need that. With Ian, I knew I wasn't going in as a victim who was going to have counselling for ever. I went in knowing that I was going to have to work very hard — sometimes I'd leave with a thumping headache, but it was the right approach for me. After seeing Ian, I can now go off and do work on my own, though I know I can come back if something isn't right, and get help where I need it.

The other thing was that I applied for this theatre director's course, which I'd wanted to do for eight or nine years but I couldn't get sponsorship. Even though I'd written a hundred and twenty letters, I couldn't get a penny. It finally came to the day when I was about to ring them up and say I couldn't do it, and I went out with a friend and we came up with the idea of asking seven hundred people to lend me ten pounds each! We tried it out on a waiter in the restaurant and it worked, and that started the ball rolling. I actually didn't believe I'd fail. I thought 'I'm loved enough by enough people to ask.' For probably the first time in my life I feel very open to giving and receiving a lot more. I feel that's a direct result of the counselling I was having. So far, I've got half the money I need for the year. Before I went into therapy, I would have taken the lack of money as confirming the fact that I didn't deserve it. Now, I thought 'I can demand this of the world and it will give it to me.' And it did.

Chapter 13

Talking to counsellors

Good counsellors often seem to know things about you that only a telepath could have discovered. At other times, their behaviour and the direction of their interest can appear totally irrational. Whilst we wouldn't like to make out that counsellors always work to a pre-set plan (many would find the idea an anathema), their behaviour is nevertheless guided by theory and trained perception which means that your counsellor's perception of a session is quite different from your own.

Most of the counsellors we spoke to were naturally unwilling to speak about their clients' problems, so the interviews tend to be far less anecdotal than the client interviews in Chapter 12. Nevertheless, their words are a rich source of insight into how the process of counselling is structured.

Where possible, our interviewees' actual words were used, although we have edited text to avoid repetition and clarify unclear points. The text you see here, as with the client interviews, has been approved by the interviewees themselves. We suggest that you use these interviews to

- provide a background and framework to the more factual and informative sections of this book
- get a sense of the counsellor's perspective to form a more rounded picture of the counselling process
- gain an idea of the process of becoming a counsellor if you consider becoming one yourself.

Charles — group work with residential clients

Charles is an Adlerian psychotherapist of many years training and experience who works with groups and individuals in a work based setting. He is a counsellor you might meet if you 'fell into the net' of social services or therapeutic residential projects.

What's the difference between therapy and counselling? At the British Association of Counselling, we've been trying to decide that for the last seven years, I think. We still can't come to any agreement as to what is counselling and what is psychotherapy, let alone agree on the distinction.

I think, for me, counselling is an activity which most people enter into through a conscious decision, being aware of what its function will be, that it will take place for a certain period of time, that it will be very contractual. Its function can be several-fold. It has a function to explore one's inner world. It has a function to seek solutions to emotional or relationship problems. It has the function to some degree to bring unconscious material into consciousness. I also see it as having a role of empowering people to act. I think it has a supportive function, a curative function. It can also have a terminal function, in terms of bereavement and working to conclusions.

It's interesting. Although one would assume that counsellors have a fair idea of what they mean by counselling, if you put two counsellors together, you never get the same ideas. I think therefore that counselling is extremely diverse in terms of the practices used. Some counsellors use very active counselling methods and some do not, and that can have quite an impact on the client. I think that to draw a distinction between the schools of thought one follows is actually much more important to the counsellor than it is to the patient!

As far as clients are concerned, I have those I see in my work setting and a small private practice. In my work setting, I have been specializing in AIDS over the past four years, as well as supervising other counsellors dealing with addiction, predominantly, alcohol and tranquiliser withdrawal. Historically, I have primarily worked in psychiatric hospitals or units dealing with a diverse range of psycho-logical presentations; anything from relationship problems to difficulties developing from acute on-set of physical illness such as a stroke, or AIDS.

The criterion for many of my clients is homelessness; I see everyone from non-English speaking people who have arrived in this country homeless to people who have been sleeping rough under Charing Cross Bridge for the past ten years, to social workers and teachers who have developed a drink problem. It's a fair mixture, with the common link of homelessness.

What I'm particularly concerned with is developing therapeutic community care rather than counselling in the more orthodox sense. I also tend to do a lot of work in terms of supervision; I do a lot of consultative work with residential workers and a lot of training for Housing Departments, Housing Associations, various residential establishments and the Directorate of the Social Services. It is a very diverse picture.

My private practice is small. I suppose the only area I haven't worked much with is children. There isn't any sort of person I would turn down — I've had patients turn up tripping on LSD, which is quite incredible. In fact, I very rarely see any patient who is totally drug-free. I would only refuse to see someone if there was some strong transference on my part which I felt would be difficult to deal with, or if I felt in some way I would be doing something in my own interest which would outweigh the benefit that the patient would get.

When I first see someone I tend to think, 'What alternatives are on offer for this person?' Will I be able to offer them something, and if so, what kind of service? I can choose between letting them have group work or individual work, and I think I make my choice intuitively. If I think I am going to get involved in certain games if I see a client one-to-one, then often I will see a group as a practical option. I see groups as a very good process to develop social skills. There is a model in my head where we start with the individual, and the healthier the individual is, the greater their involvement with an extended social network. So it's a natural progression to go from one-to-one counselling into a group situation, whereas the other way round would seem regressive. Once a client is in a group, I rarely take them out for individual work.

Particularly as I often undertake group work in residential settings, being aware of the 'incestuous' nature of residential systems, I tend to use counsellors who are not involved with the day-to-day care of the resident. Better still, have the client go out into the community and receive counselling that way rather than an in-house system.

In my work setting, groups run for an initial six-month period, at the end of this time, the group can decide to continue for a further three months. Each group has eight people and two staff members working with it. The group of eight wouldn't be together the whole time. They would only come together twice a week into those groups, for an hour-and-a half each time.

My approach is future orientated rather than past fixated. That is, we work toward a goal. It is the goal that is the important part, not the fact that you have had a traumatic experience in the past that is influencing your present behaviour in some way. I get clients to identify and prioritize their goals, and then we do active exploration of them.

My particular approach is really informed by my theoretical background. I suppose that my model of counselling is a cross between behaviourism and rational-emotional therapy. It's a lot about the way you think you will be — lots of time spent on how one talks to oneself, and how that influences your behaviour. If you can change the way you think and talk to yourself, externally, one hopes, the behaviour can begin to change. I am also interested in images and I think that the images we perceive are often very influential, although the Adlerian school of thought itself is very much word orientated.

With archetypal psychologies, symbolism and dream work are particularly interesting to me. I feel there are correlations between what Adlerians call 'early memories' and 'life style' assessment and the dreams clients choose to bring to the counselling sessions. I have also been very influenced in my counselling work by Buddhist psychology and the concept of 'emptying out', rather than taking more on board. To conclude, I would see my overall philosophy as primarily based in ego psychology, developing from a diverse mixture of schools of thought that is still growing and changing.

Westminster Pastoral Foundation trainees — long-term training for full-time work

This is drawn from a discussion with three trainees on a long-term psychoanalytically based formal counselling course, but for the sake of readability we have presented it as if it were just one person. It covers some of the issues involved in entering long-term counselling training.

I'm on the day-release course, so I've been coming for four years, half a day a week, with client work on top of that. It's been an amazing experience. Very good. I've changed a lot, and it's changed my life.

There are many routes here, so, quite apart from being with different people, our experiences are bound to be enormously different as well. According to whether you're doing the course full-time, part-time or on day release, it makes a huge difference.

The first foundation year is very intensive. We look at various aspects of group work and actual techniques in counselling, and the family and marital dimension and the social perspective. There's also a series of seminars on personality development. That's fundamental. It's a sort of spiral — you all follow similar tracks but each year you get more and more depth in the way that you look at it. We look at development right from birth until death, so you are encompassing the whole of a person and all the developmental stages.

We don't, in our case, have lectures. We have some very good practical seminars, using video, role play — good solid stuff which goes alongside the theory. In a lot of the seminars we have a structure given by the seminar leader, and then each of us does preparation and presents an introduction to the material and uses that as a basis for discussion, which is a very active way of learning. Everyone is expected to have read a chapter of a particular book or have some knowledge of it, and then it takes off into a discussion. Our seminar leader feeds into and adds to it and so on. That's how it works. So most of the seminars are quite student involved.

To start with, for the first year, when I had to do some subject or other, I was really furious because I felt it was more than I could take in at that time. If I couldn't take it in, how could I possibly help anybody else to understand it? But it's surprising what you do when you have to.

There are also role plays. The seminar leader gives us a book to read, but then we have to do some activity or some role play that allows us to get in touch with the feelings that would be around for somebody in that book. I remember the last one, about death. We did a most vivid exercise about the break, and about losing contact with another person. If you haven't experienced the death of someone close, as I haven't, it's one way of helping us to get in touch with the feelings that may be around. That whole course of seminars was really lively in that way.

I hope to finish this summer and then go on to do a final full-time membership year next year. That will be quite difficult — out of a class of twenty, only nine got on the membership course this year. I think it's not quite clear to the trainees what it is they're aiming at and what is being looked for in them. That is the uncertain area. You don't really know what criteria you're being judged by, but you do know you're being judged. You know that it's got something to do with yourself as opposed to other courses, where it's to do with your thinking or writing. On this course I am aware that the times I get most anxious about how I'm doing are those times when I feel there's nothing I can do about that except have endless years more therapy.

During the course of the year, there is plenty of time and opportunity to discuss things with your supervisor, who I think has an important role both for our training and for our work with our own clients. There's opportunity to talk during the course of the year about what areas you need to work on and what areas in our client work are shaky. So there is a way in which you can begin to look at different areas that are not quite right or need to be explored more. But the other side is, yes, decisions are made in all courses over which one does not have any control.

I will get a qualification at the end of the course, but I'm not sure how much you can distinguish between qualification and knowledge. Perhaps obtaining a qualification enables you to do certain things, or to feel that you are ready and prepared to do things. Maybe that is the difference between being on a course such as this one and doing, say, ten weeks on counselling then calling yourself a counsellor.

I hope to be able to practise other counselling when I finish, and to continue developing my own skills. I'm hoping to start a private practice at home when I've finished, because all the therapists in my area have long waiting lists so there's plenty of work to do.

Samaritans trainees — short-term training for emergency listening

This extract was taken from a discussion with three Samaritans volunteers. It offers insights into the way ordinary people can, given a short training, provide high-quality effective counselling under very difficult circumstances.

I had gone along to the Citizen's Advice Bureau to find out about voluntary work, and they suggested the Samaritans, so I went to an open evening they hold from time to time. They told us what it was like; a general chat to give you an idea of things that might come up, to let you know that you would have to go through formal training, to give you an idea of whether you would want to go through with it. I found some of the things they were saying very odd. I thought 'I couldn't do that'.

The open evening gets rid of a few people who can't go to training sessions, or haven't the commitment. They can't really tell you what it's like being a Samaritan, so they have to weed out people who still may have problems. They give you an idea of the commitment — they say that you have to do ten hours a month plus the odd night. That is your commitment, and you have to do that. That gets rid of some people too.

When I came along for the open evening, I really didn't think I'd be capable of doing it. I didn't know what they were looking for, but I didn't think I'd be suitable. They don't actually choose you that night. You decide whether you want to carry on, then you're interviewed by the Directors and they let you know within a couple of days after that whether you have been chosen or not and can go along to the training classes.

In the interview, they make you look at yourself to make sure you can stand up to the work. It's easy to say, 'It'd be nice to be a Samaritan and listen to people's problems,' but you don't think of the whole range of problems that there can be. If you've had a problem, you have to think what happens if someone comes on the phone who has exactly that problem, or the problem of the person you've just broken up with. You need to be able to sit and listen objectively. They make you think about yourself, because they don't know whether or not you can cope.

I didn't think I would get accepted, because I didn't know if I was the right sort of person. When I had an interview, I thought I wouldn't get accepted, and, even if I did get accepted, I didn't know if it would be for me. It's a bit like going for a job interview. Even when you get the letter, you are under no obligation. If you don't want to go back and start the classes, there is no obligation. When I joined I thought it was an interesting exercise, without even thinking about whether I wanted to be a Samaritan.

When you go into the training, it's sixteen hours spread over eight weeks. The main way of teaching is through doing role plays. You have two people, a trainer who plays a caller on the telephone, and you, sitting back to back. You can't hang up, so you've got to keep it going. You're not only thinking about the phone, the caller, you've got the whole class there to worry about. That's when you start thinking, 'Will I cope?' You'll be faced with something which you've never really had to think about before. Afterwards, you all discuss it.

Sometimes, the trainer will set a trap. He might be talking about a loss, and you think it must be his dog, or somebody close to him, but it turns out to be something like a screwdriver that he's lost. But if you do fall into it, what everyone does is laugh. Often you're the first one to see what you did wrong, or the other trainees will tell you. Then you talk through it — what would you have done, what would you suggest? But they can't tell you exactly what to do, because there's never a right answer.

What they're getting you ready for is to expect the unexpected, to train you to come across situations you may never have thought of, because that is going to happen. They don't want you to go to the phone thinking, 'I've been through all these various situations, I'm fine now.' When it comes to it, it may be something different again — they can't actually tell you what's right or wrong.

Also, the trainers are working to keep you within the range of listening rather than giving advice but there are different sorts of listening in order to bring out the problems. The one thing you are told to do is ask the suicide question each time — to check if people have thought of killing themselves, and to answer the phone, 'Samaritans, can I help you?' But apart from that, people's styles vary a lot. Some are chatty, others listen. There are all sorts of questions to ask and everyone has their own technique. Some callers respond better to one person than to another; some prefer talking to men rather than to women. What the trainers try to do is to get you to think about how you would cope with each situation, what technique you would use in order to try to get people to talk.

There is the question of how do you cope with an upsetting call. You can't talk about a caller at home, but you can talk out a problem with other Samaritans. If someone has had an awful phone call, the other Samaritans rally round and give the same sort of support that a family would.

We are told right from the start that you have to talk about it to someone and not go home until you can cope. Even if you are crying your eyes out for hours, and drinking endless cups of tea, it doesn't actually matter, nobody is going to laugh at you. Everybody always gives everybody else a lot of support. Within a couple of minutes of talking to somebody on the phone, there's always somebody at my side saying 'Are you all right?' which is really nice. Also they can make you laugh ever so quickly.

At the end of the training, you're not automatically a Samaritan. You still have another interview to find out whether you still want to do it, and whether they want you. You become a helper, on probation for six months always working with an experienced Samaritan, then a full Samaritan.

When you find yourself on the end of a real live phone line for the first time, you're always terrified, your heart's going and you get butterflies. I've not met anyone who didn't say that. The first time I was shaking—but even now, my heart beats. There's always a little jump, when the phone goes, until you find out what it's all about. Then it might be someone who rings straight off—we call it an 'instant disconnection', but you don't know until it happens. If it is, when they put the phone down, at first you wonder if you've answered the phone too abruptly. But you soon come to realize that they might have been too frightened to talk to you, or have got what they needed just by knowing they could ring the Samaritans.

After every call, I say to myself, 'Did I say the right things?' You get less self-conscious as you get used to working with other people in the room, and you get used to other people listening in—not to the call but to check that you're all right. As I said, you're taught not to bottle it up if you do get upset afterwards. There's no such thing as putting on a brave face—they don't thank you for doing that.

Not everybody rings in because they're suicidal. A lot of people who call *are* depressed, but people phone for any reason—because they're lonely, or confused, or because they're really happy and couldn't tell anybody. They need to get it out, tell somebody about it. Some ring just to talk to somebody anonymous about something they can't share.

It is tempting to give advice, but it doesn't work like that. You can just talk through the options with them, and consider each one with them, and they just work it out for themselves with you to talk to.

Of course, we also work face to face, though we don't do much of it. I'm terrified of it. I think the person who wants to come and sit down and talk to you face to face is terribly brave, because obviously there is a chance that you might see that person again, or they might see you. So, however terrified I am, I think that the other person must be more terrified. At least if you are face-to-face though, you can put an arm round someone, whereas on the phone, I find it really difficult that I can't do that.

Also, with a face-to-face, it's probable that you will find out what has happened to people, whereas with a phone call, you don't. I find the most difficult thing when I put the phone down is that I don't know what's happened. Unless people ring back, you never know. It is lovely when people do ring or write back to tell you when they've got through their problems, but they mostly don't.

I've spoken to people who have been Samaritans for years, and still jump when the phone goes, because you don't know what's going to be on the other end of it. No amount of training is going to help you with an unknown call. When you think it can, then it's time to leave.

It's not what you say, it's the fact that you're there.

Rose — eclectic humanistic psychotherapy and counselling

Rose is an eclectic psychotherapist, drawing on many of the different schools and styles within the Growth movement. She offers one-to-one psychotherapy and counselling and runs groups. You would be most likely to find her through the recommendation of a friend or neighbour.

I first got into 'counselling' and self-development when I was about ten or eleven years old in a bid to educate myself—I had questions about sex and so on which weren't being answered. I went to the local library and found some adult books which I couldn't get out on children's tickets, so I used to sneak them out in my school bag, read them and take them back. It started then.

I kept reading, and, when I was in my early twenties, I went to an evening class course called 'Living with our Tension'. We did some Yoga, and smatterings of things which gave me a taste to go further. Then I became much more interested in self-development when I became pregnant and began reading books about touch and contact. From there I went on to the Natural Childbirth Trust and then I formed a group at home of people who had been involved in the NCT.

Then I began to get more involved with consciousness raising and founded a centre for women in the local community. We began to get a sense that feelings were coming up in the group that we wanted to cope with. We got in touch with the Women's Therapy Centre in London and learned about self-help therapy. Around that time, I heard about Co-

Counselling. I contacted a woman who taught Co-Counselling and she came along and gave us a basic, fundamentals course in it. At the end of the course, we did something on fantasy, what we wanted of ourselves. One of the things I dared to hope was that I would be able to teach Co-Counselling. That was a big fantasy for me at that time, but the seed was planted.

From that time, through the Co-Counselling network, I started to set up workshops; I set up a rebirthing workshop, for example. I also observed a teacher during a fundamentals course in order to learn more, did a Co-Counselling teachers' course, co-taught at the women's centre, then did a fundamentals course on my own. That was a very big step for me, particularly to get a big group working together.

Then I heard about the Facilitator Styles course at Surrey University and got on a course in North London, which was quite amazing for me at that time. That was one day a week plus one weekend a month which was quite a lot for me to negotiate with young children and a partner who wasn't too keen on the idea. I did the course because I thought that I didn't have enough skills; the course gave me a taste of different types of humanistic skills such as Gestalt 'cushion' work, visualization, body awareness, breathing, group dynamics, games, peer work, negotiation, 'owning' stuff and how to do that, and so on and so forth. It was all relevant to individual one-to-one work and also for group work. It gave me more confidence and experience to work with individuals.

From there, I found a psychotherapy course which involved a more spiritual dimension — meditation, breathing, archetypes, chants, songs, dances and many things which I felt I wanted to incorporate into the humanistic side. I heard about Biodynamic therapy which seemed to incorporate body work and the spiritual dimension too, so I did some work with that, which I'm still doing at the moment.

There's a church in Piccadilly where they do crisis counselling for people who come in off the street and I did some voluntary counselling there. That was quite a training because they have all sorts of people there, people who are on drugs, schizophrenics, people who are deeply distressed. It was supervised, so it was a very good experience. It was very different from anything I'd done before, but everything

I'd done before helped it.

I've got a small practice at home now, since that time, doing one-to-one sessions, seeing individuals and couples for psychotherapy and counselling. I've also done some training with the Parent Network whose aims are to help parents improve their relationships with children.

In terms of what I'm doing now, I'm running groups — a parent group at my home, one-to-one clients with individual and crystal therapy and counselling. I've also just been up to Wales to visit a community, helping them to look at the group dynamics which involved their children as well. I'd like to do more of that, helping with the interpersonal issues. A wandering gypsy facilitator. . .

My work with groups, which I run at home, is varied; the parent network, Co-Counselling, self-discovery groups. The basic aim for me is to assist people in discovering their strengths and developing self-confidence and their ability to share that with people. People in my groups want to relate and communicate with each other on a deeper level, what their expectations are, how they want to be, and what they need. Then I would offer exercises and group skills that they can experience — perhaps role play, games, massage, listening to each other, depending on what the group need was at the time. I bring in music, meditation, touch, contact, verbal exchange, so that it becomes an all-round experience.

People in my groups usually commit themselves weekly for about three hours for several weeks, with a possibility of following up with a networking group. I'd expect, and have, a regular strong commitment of people coming weekly. I advertise in the Co-Counselling directory and have put some cards up in wholefood shops. I did teach evening classes for three years so people came from there directly. I occasionally advertise in local listings magazines. Most of my people come through word of mouth.

I do it for personal satisfaction and personal growth for me and others. I feel very privileged. I'm learning all the time.

Diane — hospital counselling

Diane is a hospital counsellor working within the NHS. She also has a small private practice. You would be most likely to meet her as part of the team that works with you if you have to go into hospital for a treatment that could affect you emotionally as well as physically.

I originally did a psychology degree, and decided after that to go into social work with a psychiatric bias. Then I did my postgraduate social work training and went into psychiatric social work. At the same time as I was doing that, I did a year's basic individual counselling training with the Westminster Pastoral Foundation. I also did two years with the Institute of Group Analysis and some short courses, including some bereavement counselling. I've recently done some further training at Goldsmith's College, and I'm just launching into a psychotherapeutic training with the British Association of Psychotherapy. Along the way, I've had psychotherapy myself, and that's a requirement anyway for the BAP training.

I've probably worked mainly on a humanistic basis, though quite eclectically. I don't work with one school, because of the different kinds of training I've had, and because, doing group work, you use a variety of different models. I think as I move more towards psychotherapy, I'm moving more towards a psychodynamic, analytical way of working, and exploring that for myself, using it with my private patients.

The counselling I do slots neatly into two types. I work in a hospital, counselling women who come in to a colposcopy clinic, women who have had abnormal smears. I see them when they come for their first session, those who come back for further visits, and then I see those who have more severe disease when they begin the therapy and through until they begin to recover. I also work with groups; I've run psychiatric patient groups, I've worked with depressed women for some time using assertiveness training for confidence building. More recently I've had a group of young male cardiac patients — that was a confidence-building exercise, building group support so that we could use each other's resources.

I've been working at the hospital for seven years, but my work has changed a lot over that time. I was employed originally as a medical social worker, to work on the gynaecological ward and the medical ward, and with women who were considering abortions. Over the years, my interest in gynaecology grew and I was much more interested in dealing with that. Along the way I became involved with the Hysterectomy Support Group, did some counselling with them and did some training of their volunteer counsellors. Gradually, I moved away from doing general social work to doing counselling work.

I do very short-term work with the hospital patients — I see them at the most two or three times, assessing them, offering them time and space to look through the feelings they have at that time, offering them attention where they haven't had it before. The model is very different from psychotherapy, where you would expect to see someone over months or years, where you are doing far more exploratory work with them.

The work I do in the colposcopy clinic is demanding. People see me the first time they come to the clinic; they will have had a letter beforehand with my name on it, which gives them an outline of what will happen at the clinic, why they're there. They're invited to ring me beforehand, and many do because they're in a state of panic. The first session is very much an information-giving session for them, while I'm trying to assess what is happening to each woman, how well she's coping, what she understands, how much information she wants and how much she can handle it or doesn't want to know anything about it. The first session is really very short, about twenty minutes, sometimes less than that.

We see people who are very frightened. I saw a woman yesterday who said that she had thought several times of driving her car into a wall and was terrified because she was at the time dealing with the death of a friend from cervical cancer.

I see women when they come back for results and treatment, and I'm the person who gives them the news. I work very closely with the consultant who now trusts me to do that, and we find that it works well if I tell them what's happening and counsel them at the same time. You're dealing with how much information a woman wants, what fears and fantasies she has, and how information can help those. A lot of what I'm doing is explaining and then listening and giving attention to the fears they have. I ask questions designed to bring up anxieties and then pay attention while a woman tells me what they are.

I then counsel a handful of women who need more help, either because they have cancer or because they are very frightened or have particular problems, and develop it into a full-blown counselling relationship. At that stage there's far more coming from me in the way of information, and far more coming from them about what they're feeling and how they're coping, the grief and the loss and the fear. Sexuality is a big issue for many women at this stage. I introduce it at first as an information-giving thing, because in the early stages, talking about sexuality is fairly difficult. But if I introduce it through information, then they can pick up on it if they choose to.

The other part of my work is my private practice, counselling women, referred by their GP or consultant — people who have psychosomatic illnesses, or emotional problems alongside their physical illnesses.

In my private practice, I charge £10 an hour, and see people, on the whole, weekly. I like to have a weekly contract, the same time very week, so that they feel that is their time and that won't be changed around or muddled up for them. Some of them are quite hard up, people who I've been seeing for quite some time, and who want to maintain the contact but are concerned about the money, and I see some of them fortnightly, at their request. I see people for fifty minutes to an hour — I'm not very good at stopping on time.

I see people for what I call an assessment session first of all, and they talk about what they want to get out of it. I think about whether I've got anything to offer them, and if I have, ask what sort of time they see themselves giving to it. I want them to think about the sort of commitment they're giving to it, although, of course, if they say three months and then want to do more, that's all right. We can leave it open-ended, I don't insist on a firm commitment, although I tell them what my commitment is and what I have to offer. I think a lot of people arrive for counselling not having a clue what it is, and I try to make clear what sorts of things we're going to be doing.

As with the hospital patients, for many of my patients who have psychsomatic illnesses, information about the illness is a way in. Once I've got them talking about it, I try to pick up on the unconscious feelings. I don't do a great deal of interpretation; with some patients I'm working on the transference, with the relationship between myself and them. At times, the patient sees you as representing something for them or sometimes asks what it means for them. I become very aware of my own feelings, that the material the clients bring in affects me too. I want them to recognize what these feelings are, and make the connections so that they come to their own realizations about what's going on.

That's a change for me, doing that, from the more client-centred counselling I used to do. Interpretive therapy is very different, though I don't say that one is more valuable than the other. What difference does the method make to the client? I think that the psychodynamic style feeds the client less, is more facilitative and supportive, helps them to get the answers for themselves.

Why do I do it? For me, it's endlessly fascinating; demanding but satisfying. The problems that arise, the situations are always different and endlessly fascinating. It sounds pretentious to say I want to help, but it's true. I don't think I would want to do anything else.

Section 3

The possibilities

Chapter 14
Consumer guide — issues

While increasing numbers of people seek counselling out of a general desire for self-development, the starting point for most people entering counselling is a specific issue, a trigger which moves them towards seeking help. It is these issues which most often decide the sort of counselling we aim for, and therefore dictate the first place we turn to for help.

How to use this chapter

The main body of this chapter lists possible starting points for counselling. It is not an exhaustive list but it certainly covers the most usual ones. For each, we outline what the issues may be and give some indication of the ways in which counselling can help. We say, where relevant, whether NHS counselling is usually available. Often, we use as an example a typical organization which specializes in each particular issue. Where we do this, we are not suggesting that this organization is the only one of use to you, and that other similar organizations are less effective; we are merely choosing one out of the many available to give you an example of what is on offer. Equally, the listings at the end of each entry are not exhaustive, but merely a range of starting points.

Please note that a listing in this chapter does not mean that we recommend, endorse or take responsibility for any organization or individual.

Abortion

Abortion counselling deals with your emotions before and after an abortion. Before any termination of pregnancy, whether performed privately or on the National Health Service, you should be offered a chance to talk through whether both partners are totally convinced that this is the right thing to do. If you aren't offered it, ask for it. As with all counselling, get a counsellor who is affirmative of how you feel, not trying to persuade you otherwise — as anti-abortion agencies have a reputation for doing.

Post-abortion depression is also common, and you should set up counselling for yourself if you have even the mildest of kick-backs afterwards. The Family Planning Association, for example, is best known for its contraceptive advice, but many branches also offer advice, support and counselling referral for women who seek or who have had an abortion. In view of the political nature of the subject, you may want to opt for abortion counselling with a feminist perspective, in which case contacting your local women's centre may be your best starting point.

British Pregnancy Advisory Service
Austy Manor
Wootton Wawen
Solihull B95 6BX
056 79 3225
(Counselling on pregnancy, contraception, infertility and abortion)

Brook Advisory Centres
Look in your local telephone directory or contact them at:
153a East Street
London SE17 2SD
071 708 1234
(Counselling for young people on contraception, abortion, etc.)

Family Planning Association
27-35 Mortimer Street
London W1N 7RJ
071 636 7866
(Advice, information and referral.)

Pregnancy Advisory Service
11-13 Charlotte Street
London W1P 1HD
071 637 8962
(Advice and information on pregnancy, fertility-related issues
and AIDS. Referral for abortion.)

Women's Health and Reproductive Rights Information Centre
52-54 Featherstone Street
London EC1Y 8RT
071 251 6580 (Open Monday, Wednesday, Thursday, Friday,
11am-5pm)
(General referral and information)

Children by Choice
237 Lutwyche Road
Windsor
Queensland 4030
07 357 5377

AIDS

Whether you are HIV-positive or have full-blown AIDS; or
are close to someone who is, you will need support during
the diagnosis and throughout any subsequent illness or
bereavement. This may not only take the form of supportive counselling but also practical advice, information and
help in areas such as health care, housing and finance.

The Terrence Higgins Trust, the first AIDS-supportive
agency in Britain, points out in its literature that you should
at first confide only in counsellors who have been specially
trained to deal with the issues HIV and AIDS raise and
whose confidentiality you are sure of, as 'knowing you are
at risk can make people react badly because of ignorance
or prejudice'. Most AIDS counsellors are at present attached
to organizations such as telephone help-lines, hospitals and
referral agencies. The number of private counsellors who
specialize in AIDS counselling is currently low, but increasing.

Details of AIDS counsellors can usually be obtained from
your local Gay Helpline (qv) or through the Terrence Higgins Trust Helpline from 3pm to 10pm daily. Most AIDS

counselling, except that through private counsellors, is free — although most groups are also voluntary, so need donations. The Terrence Higgins Trust also offers counselling for the 'worried well' who may be concerned about their susceptibility to AIDS.

Body Positive
071 373 9124 (7-10pm, helpline)
071 835 1045 (Office hours for business and other enquiries)

Terrence Higgins Trust
BM AIDS
London WC 1N 3XX
081 242 1010 (Helpline)

London Institute for the Study of Human Sexuality
10 Warwick Road
Earl's Court
London SW5 9UH
071 373 0901 (Ansaphone)

National AIDS Helpline
PO Box 1577   and   PO Box 5000
Camden Town   Glasgow G12 9BL
London NW1 3DW
0800 567123

Pregnancy Advisory Service
11-13 Charlotte Street
London W1P 1HD
071 637 8962

Alcoholism

There are a number of NHS approaches to treating alcoholism, as well as a variety of private methods. These range from purely medical treatments to intensive residential drying-out courses which combine physical and emotional support.

The best-known organization is, of course, Alcoholics Anonymous, which combines group support with a comprehensive philosophy of life. Alcoholics Anonymous is so called because it guarantees anonymity for its members. It is totally self-supporting and does not rely on outside help, dues or fees. There are 2,200 local groups in Great Britain which offer regular meetings where members can receive emotional support from each other on the day-to-day problems of not drinking. Alcoholics Anonymous 'does not offer any practical help to members, but helps the alcoholic stay sober so that he can get things for himself'.

To contact Alcoholics Anonymous, look in your local telephone directory. Phones will be manned by volunteers who will answer questions and put you in touch with local groups. If there is no local telephone service for your area, phone the General Service Office of the AA on the number given below.

Alcoholics Anonymous
PO Box 1
Stonebow House
Stonebow
York YO1 2NJ
0904 644026

Richmond Fellowship for Community Mental Health
8 Addison Road
London W14 8DL
071 603 6373
(Therapeutic communities for, among others, alcoholics)

Alcoholics Anonymous
127 Edwin Street
Croydon
New South Wales 2132
02 799 1199

Bereavement

Friends and relatives will often help immediately after a bereavement, but you may find that you also need long-term expert help. Many agencies and individual counsellors offer bereavement counselling, to help you come to terms with the death of someone close to you and work through natural feelings of anger, guilt and betrayal.

One key agency is Cruse. It 'offers to help all bereaved

people wherever they live, whatever their age, nationality and belief'. It has branches throughout the country which offer home counselling, social meetings, advice on practical matters and a series of leaflets and fact sheets, many of which are free with the membership fee. Cruse headquarters will give you the number and address of your local branch.

Compassionate Friends
6 Denmark Street
Bristol BS1 5DQ
0272 292 778
(An organization for bereaved parents offering friendship and understanding to other bereaved parents)

Cot Death Research and Support for Bereaved Parents
8a Alexandra Parade
Weston Super Mare BS23 1TQ
0836 219010 and 779779/0934 413333 and 510230
(Offers counselling and counselling training.)

Cruse
Cruse House
126 Sheen Road
Richmond TW9 1UR
081 940 4818

Gay Bereavement Project
Unitarian Rooms
Hoop Lane
London NW11 8BS
081 455 8894 (Ansaphone, 7-12pm)
(Help and support after the death of a same-sex partner.)

Stillbirth and Neonatal Death Society (SANDS)
28 Portland Place
London W1N 4DE
071 436 5881

Cancer

There are many nationwide cancer counselling agencies and a number of organizations which run local groups to provide support right from the time you (or someone close to you) has the first tests. These agencies provide practical advice and emotional counselling in a number of forms, ranging from telephone support, to cancer centres which provide drop-in groups and home visitors.

BACUP, for example, is a nationwide cancer counselling agency which was started by Vicki Clement-Jones, herself a cancer sufferer. It provides initial telephone counselling and information using counsellors who are all trained nurses with special expertise in cancer issues. BACUP are also in the process of developing face-to-face counselling services. Their service is free and confidential.

BACUP
121/123 Charterhouse Street
London EC1M 6AA
071 608 1661 (5 lines — Patient information service)
0800 181199 (Freephone service)
071 608 1038 (Face-to-face counselling service)

Cancer Help Centre
Grove House
Cornwallis Grove
Clifton
Bristol BS8 4PG
0272 743216
(Holistic centre for cancer patients.)

Cancer Information and Support Society
14 Herbeton Avenue
Hunters Hill
New South Wales 2110
02 817 1912

Career Guidance

There are arguments against considering career guidance as true counselling at all. At its best, however, career guidance offers similar support to other forms of counselling, along with the information — and certainly some clients we talked to spoke of receiving both insight and change from their sessions. Career counselling is one of the more 'generative' counselling services — often it is not sought in answer to a problem, but in order to fulfil your potential.

Career guidance can be obtained through your Local Education Authority's Careers Service, which offers guidance interviews to school leavers and their parents, and then subsequent further guidance to people of all ages when they are considering a career change or coping with problems of redundancy or redeployment. Private career counselling can be obtained from a number of careers guidance agencies and individual consultants. They often involve sophisticated (and usually expensive) psychological testing. One career counsellor we interviewed was at least as concerned to offer emotional support and insight for his clients as he was to advise.

CEPEC Ltd
Jermyn Street
London SW1Y 6NY
071 930 0322
(Training in work counselling skills and career development counselling.)

CHAT (Counselling, Help and Advice Together)
Royal College of Nursing
20 Cavendish Square
London W1H 0AB
071 629 3870
(Specialist and personal counselling for nurses.)

Employee Advisory Resource
Brunel Science Park
Kingston Lane
Uxbridge UB8 3PQ
0895 71135

FOCUS (Forum for Occupational Counselling and Unemployment Services Ltd)
Northside House
Mount Pleasant
Barnet
EN4 9EB
081 441 9300
(Career change, redundancy, retirement, crisis counselling and employee assistance programmes.)

Child abuse

Currently, the violent or sexual abuse of children, or at any rate its discovery, is on the increase. In cases such as these both the children and adults involved in the situation will need help; often this comes after a crisis, when the social services take over and provide care for children and varyingly effective forms of support for adults. However, long before things come to a crisis point, counselling can help. Telephone counselling services such as Childline can give immediate support to children, while organizations such as the NSPCC can provide long-term 'preventative and therapeutic help to families.'

If you feel that you, or someone you know, is in danger of beginning to abuse their children, then you will get support rather than condemnation if you contact the NSPCC, who understand the problems involved.

If you were abused as a child, and are distressed about it now, you can go to any of the general counselling services we mention, or contact specialist agencies such as those which offer counselling for incest victims. The Incest Crisis Line offers 'a sympathetic listening service run by people who have been incest victims in the past.'

Childline
Freepost 1111
London N1 0BR
0800 1111 (Freephone)

Incest Crisis Line
PO Box 32
Northolt
Middlesex
UB5 4JC
081 890 4732

NCH (National Children's Homes) Carelines (support for families)
85 Highbury Park
London N5 1UD
071 226 2033
(For local Careline numbers, contact Directory Enquiries.)

NSPCC
67 Saffron Hill
London EC1N 8RS
071 242 1626

Incest Survivors Association
Ste 7
85 Stirling Street
Perth
Western Australia 6000
09 227 8745

Child Abuse Prevention Service
33 Bundock Street
Randwick
New South Wales 2031
02 344 7646

Couples counselling

What used to be called 'marriage guidance' is now recognized to be needed by any couple, married or not. Equally, there is no need to wait until your relationship is on the rocks before seeking a counsellor.

The national organization for couples counselling used to be called the National Marriage Guidance Council, but is now called *Relate*. They are heavily oversubscribed, so you may need to wait a while before a counsellor can take you on their list. You can work alone, with your partner, or in a group, usually for between an hour to an hour and a half per week. You are asked to 'contribute what you can afford'. Directory Enquiries will give you the number of your local centre. Many private counsellors, like ourselves, also work with couples.

Catholic Marriage Advisory Council
1 Blythe Mews
Blythe Road
London W14 ONW
071 371 1341

Jewish Marriage Guidance Council
23 Ravenshurst Avenue
London NW4 4EE
081 203 6311

Marriage Counselling Scotland
26 Frederick Street
Edinburgh EH2 2JR
031 225 5006

Relate (National Marriage Guidance Council)
Herbert Gray College
Little Church Street
Rugby
Warwickshire CV21 3AP
0788 573241

Tavistock Institute of Marital Studies
Tavistock Centre
120 Belsize Lane
London NW3 5BA
071 435 7111

Australian Association of Marriage and Family Counsellors
41 Cabarita Road
Armadale
Western Australia 6112

Culturally based counselling

There are many organizations which specialize in issues that are specific to one culture, or the problem of cultural adaption. In addition, of course, there are counselling agencies which offer counselling by people from your particular culture, who may be able to understand your view of the world more accurately than indigenous counsellors.

Asian Family Counselling Service
Equity Chambers   and 74 The Avenue
40 Piccadilly   London W13 8LB
Bradford   081 997 5749
BD1 3NN
0274 720 486
(Counselling with cultural awareness.)

NAFSIYAT — the Inter-Cultural Therapy Centre
278 Seven Sisters Road
Finsbury Park
London N4 2HY
071 263 4130

Depression

You may first realize that you are depressed when you go to the doctor with a number of physical symptoms, and are prescribed some of the chemical methods (tranquilizers and anti-depressants) of suppressing depression symptoms. Your doctor may also offer you counselling through the NHS, usually in a group situation and often only if your depression is severe.

You may, however, want to build your own support system through counselling organizations or private counsellors. If so, you need to decide which approach will suit you best, as almost all schools of counselling are happy to treat depression in their own particular way. You may also need to make a choice between taking the prescribed drugs and getting counselling. Many counsellors (including us) don't consider it appropriate to counsel someone who is under the influence of emotion-blockers. Sadly, despite the high incidence of depression today, we could find no organization specializing in the condition, though many of the more generalized ones reported working largely with depressed clients.

The Samaritans
17 Uxbridge Road
Slough SL1 1SN
0753 32713

Samaritans Australia
Consult your local
area phone directory.

MIND
22 Harley Street
London W1
071 637 0741

Lifeline
148 Lonsdale Street
Melbourne
Victoria 3000
03 662 1677

Drug abuse

If you approach your doctor with a drug abuse problem, you will be offered medical and emotional help through the NHS. There are, however, a number of more wide-ranging support agencies which also offer legal help and general welfare advice. Many individual counsellors give drug counselling, but it is more usual for those seeking to come off drugs to choose an organization or centre which offers medical and practical help as well as emotional support.

Release is a national organization which employs a team of trained drugs and legal advisors to give both practical advice and counselling. They work over the phone and are also happy to see callers with problems. They are particularly committed to 'the welfare of people using drugs' and involve themselves with legal problems, as well as giving referral to appropriate local treatment and counselling services. Their service is totally confidential and they promise never to disclose information about their callers. They are funded by grants and fees from training and consultancy work, and so their services are free, but donations are always welcome.

Release
169 Commercial Street
London E1 6BW
071 377 5905 (10am-6pm)
071 603 8654 (24 hour helpline)

Richmond Fellowship for Community Mental Health
8 Addison Road
London W14 8DL
071 603 6373/4/5
(Residential community offering support to, among others, drug users)

Association of Drug Referral Centres Ltd
91 Pittswater Road
Manly
New South Wales 2095
02 977 2197

Drug Research and Rehabilitation Association Inc
109 St George's Terrace
Perth
Western Australia 6000
09 321 3191

Eating disorders

Both overeating and undereating are problems when taken to excess. Nowadays you can get counselling for eating disorders such as anorexia nervosa and bulimia nervosa from a number of sources. Your GP may well be able to refer you for NHS counselling, although reports we had suggested that this tends to consist of a mixture of hospitalization, controlled feeding and simple listening.

There are also a number of specialist organizations to help you take on a more relaxed attitude to eating. Eating disorder counselling is often also done by individual private counsellors, many of them former sufferers. The Maisner Method for compulsive eaters and bulimics was founded by Paulette Maisner, herself a compulsive eater for many years. It combines a detailed questionnaire about your eating habits with a sensible eating plan, guidance and occasional specialist workshops. Although a great deal of the Maisner Method is concerned with information giving, it also offers support; 'you can telephone the Centre as many times as you want...' and where necessary, you are referred for specialist change work on your particular problem. The Maisner Method is a private service and charges fees.

Lifespace
100 Gloucester Road
London SW7 4AU
071 584 8819

The Maisner Method
PO Box 464
Hove
East Sussex
BN3 2BN
0273 729818

Family therapy

If the issue you are dealing with is one that involves or affects your whole family you may well look for family therapy. A counsellor will work with one or more members of a family individually or in a group in order to help the stress thay are all under. The Institute of Family Therapy suggests such counselling for 'families experiencing psychological, behavioural and relationship problems.'

We would recommend that you try family therapy particularly if one member of your family (adult or child) is acting in an odd or distressed way, but be warned — you may find yourself being expected to take your share of responsibility for what is going on, and you could find this threatening. Family therapy nearly always takes place within an organization, and is usually funded by either the NHS or local authority. We know of no national register of family therapists, so you will need to search locally: look out for anything with a name like: Family Consultation Centre; Child and Family Consultation Centre; Child Guidance Clinic; Child Psychiatric Clinic.

Some local branches of MIND run family therapy clinics.

MIND
22 Harley Street
London W1 2ED
071 637 0741

For parent support and training groups, contact:

The Parent Network
44 Caversham Road
London NW5
071 485 8535

Counselling for particular family situations, such as one-parent families or families with step-parents is rarely available, despite the very particular problems these raise. We tracked down just two relevant organizations.

Asian Family Counselling Service
74 The Avenue
London
W13 8LB
081 997 5749

National Step-family Association
72 Willesden Lane
London NW6 7TA
071 372 0844 (Office) (Monday-Friday, 9am-5pm)
071 372 0846 (Counselling Service)

Gay or lesbian issues

Having non-standard sexual preferences is still liable to provoke discrimination and prejudice in society. So, whether you are just coming out or already meeting day-to-day problems, you may need support. The usual entry point will be the gay telephone help-line in your area, which you will be able to find through Directory Enquiries or your local library. They will be able to refer you either to a gay counselling service, if you live in a city, or to individual counsellors. We would repeat the point made earlier in the book, and taken from *The Lavender Couch*, that it is much more important to find a counsellor who is affirmative of your sexual preferences than it is to find one who actively shares them; in some places, the latter may be impossible to find. If you cannot track down your local gay community, contact the London Lesbian and Gay Switchboard (071 837 7324).

Gay Bereavement Project
Unitarian Rooms
Hoop Lane
London NW11 8BS
081 455 8894 (Manned 7-12pm, Ansaphone otherwise with direction on to counsellors)
(Help and support after the death of a same-sex partner.)

Jewish Lesbian and Gay Helpline
BM Jewish Helpline
London WC1N 3XX
081 706 3123 (Manned Monday and Thursday 7-10pm, Ansaphone otherwise)

Gay and Lesbian Counselling Service
33 Wellington Street
Chippendale
New South Wales 2008
02 319 2799

Gay Counselling Service Association Inc
PO Box 459
North Adelaide
South Australia 5004
08 232 0794

General unhappiness

As we mentioned at the start of the chapter, you can feel generally anxious, depressed or unhappy without being able to identify a specific issue about which you need help.

For emergency help, you will probably need a telephone help-line of some sort. The Samaritans, contrary to many popular myths, is not just for those who want to commit suicide. We spoke to a number of people who had felt bad, particularly during the night hours, and who had been greatly helped by the Samaritan volunteers. The Samaritans also offer a 'befriending' service, where volunteers make contact with callers and offer them a listening ear.

In the long term your best bet is either to find an individual private counsellor or a local support group, or learn to Co-Counsel. Private counsellors are normally the most expensive of these options, though many training schools (see Chapter 15) offer sessions with their trainees at reduced rates.

Co-Counselling Phoenix
5 Victoria Road
Sheffield S10 2DJ
0742 686371
(Classes in and literature on Cathartic counselling including Co-Counselling.)

Samaritans
17 Uxbridge Road
Slough SL1 1SN
0753 32713

Handicap or disabilities

Physical handicap or disability may well need practical or medical support, but also demands emotional supports. Shockingly, this is rarely available to patients or their families through state channels, and so a number of privately funded bodies exist which not only provide practical help but can also refer you on for counselling. Your best starting point will be to track down the specialist organization for your particular handicap or disability through the usual channels of library, telephone book or hospital.

Outsiders Club
PO Box 4ZB
London W1A WZB
071 499 0900 (Manned 2-7pm each day, Ansaphone otherwise)
(Counselling around disablement issues.)

SPOD (Association to aid the Sexual and Personal Relationship of People with a Disability)
286 Camden Road
London N7 OBJ
071 607 8851

Hysterectomy

Losing your ability to bear children may be a conscious, or an unavoidable decision, but it may also be a trigger for unhappiness and depression for you or your partner — remember that both partners may need counselling about their common loss of childbearing potential.

Both before and after a hysterectomy, most hospitals now offer counselling of some form, although as with all NHS services, it is usually overstretched and therefore may not last as long as you would wish. The Hysterectomy Support Group provides telephone support and counselling for women before and after hysterectomy. This network is made up of women who themselves have had hysterectomies and because of this, it is particularly useful. Many private counsellors, usually women, also offer support on hysterectomy as well as the issues around stillbirth and miscarriage.

Hysterectomy Support Group
11 Henryson Road
Brockley
London SE4 1HL
081 690 5987 (Ansaphone)

Illness

Bearing in mind that any illness may be emotionally as well as physically debilitating, and that the list of officially recognized psychosomatic ailments grows daily, there are shockingly few NHS counselling agencies for the ill. Hospitals will offer counselling but, owing to the shortage of funds, this is often only for the terminally ill, or if you are willing to see the representative of a particular religious faith. However, organizations to offer physical support to those with major illnesses such as cancer (qv), and multiple sclerosis, often include in their services some sort of emotional support. These organizations are far too numerous for us to mention in full here, but you can find out more from your hospital, community nurse or the Citizen's Advice Bureau.

Phobias

A phobia is an incapacitating fear of something; common ones include fear of open spaces, insects or heights. They are often caused by a single, traumatic incident, and result in total panic when faced with the trigger. There are a number of approaches to phobias, some include gradual habituation and desensitization to the thing you are afraid of, others tackle the problem by building up confidence and self-esteem through support groups. Modern visualization methods can often cure a phobia in a single session; sadly we have yet to track down an organization in this country that uses them.

It is now more and more recognized that phobias are real and cannot simply be overcome by 'pulling yourself together'. So the NHS may, in your area, offer phobia counselling and it is worth mentioning your problem to your GP. Equally, voluntary support groups, often based round a single phobia, have been set up in some big cities, and Directory Enquiries or your Citizen's Advice Bureau may be able to give you a contact point. Phobic Action, for example, is a network of self-help support groups, centred particularly around agoraphobia, which also gives referrals to qualified private practitioners.

Phobic Action
Greater London House
547/551 High Road
Leytonstone
London E11 4PB
081 558 6012

Rape counselling

Directly after rape has occurred, ringing a rape crisis centre can give you practical information and advice on how to cope; it will also give you the support of someone used to coping in this sort of crisis, and who will affirm your distress even if others react negatively. Ringing Directory Enquiries will give you the number of your nearest Rape Crisis Centre, which will usually be open 24 hours a day. Even if this is in a town some way away, ring them if you can and get advice.

Later, you may need more long-term support. Many counselling agencies such as the London Rape Crisis Centre, and many individual counsellors, offer ways of working through the negative emotions which go with being raped. It may be important to work with a counsellor of your gender on these issues, at least to begin with.

London Rape Crisis Centre
PO Box 69
London WC1X 9NJ
071 278 3956 (Ansaphone)
071 837 1600
(24-hour counselling line for women.)

Survivors
Panther House
38 Mount Pleasant
London WC1X OAP
071 833 3737 (Helpline) (Tuesday and Thursday evenings)
(Advice and information on the sexual abuse of men.)

Religion

Religion can be a comfort, but it can also be a source of conflict. We have included it in this list of issues because we found that it is often a subject for counselling, and also because counselling with a specifically religious approach can be particularly helpful to many people.

If you are having problems integrating your religion with the other things that are happening in your life at the moment, you may choose to go for counselling to someone who is *not* of your religious persuasion. It can be difficult to get such counselling on the NHS, so you may well need to go to a private counsellor. You may also find it difficult to identify which counsellors have the approach to religious issues that you want. Check this with them when you make contact.

It could be, however, that you need someone with just your religious background, maybe someone with a specific religious affiliation, with whom you can feel comfortable. Many religious disciplines have a counselling programme and of course many religious ministers are trained or experienced in counselling. There are also agencies which offer counselling to those in the religious life, who may need support because of that very fact.

Dympna Centre
60 Grove End Road
London NW8 9NH
071 286 6107
(Support for those in religious life)
Heronbrook House International Therapeutic Centre for Clergy and Religions
Bakers Lane
Knowle
Solihull BT3 8PW
0564 776214/776215

Sexuality

Because our sexuality is such an intimate issue, it is often impossible to turn to friends, let alone partners, when we have issues around sex. Counselling offers the ideal solution.

There *is* NHS counselling for sexual issues, although it is often based on a medical model, so you could, as one woman we spoke to did, find your unwillingness to make love being explained away as a muscle dysfunction. Since many sexual issues are inextricably linked with relationships, Relate can help you work out such issues within the context of couples counselling. (You do not have to counsel with your partner in order to have counselling with Relate.) There are also a number of private counselling organizations which specialize in sexual problems, and many individual counsellors do. The Association of Sexual and Marital Therapists do not themselves offer counselling, but will give you information on the availability of marital and sexual therapy both in the NHS and the private sector if you send them a stamped self-addressed envelope.

Association of Sexual and Marital Therapists
PO Box 62
Sheffield
S10 3TS

Brooke Advisory Centres
153a East Street
London SE17 2SD
071 708 1234
(Twenty centres in seven cities offering help to young people.)

Family Planning Association
27-35 Mortimer Street
London W1N 7RJ
071 636 7866

London Institute for the Study of Human Sexuality
10 Warwick Road
Earl's Court
London SW5 9UH
071 373 0901 (Ansaphone)

Marriage Counselling Scotland
26 Frederick Street
Edinburgh EH2 2JR
031 225 5006

Relate (National Marriage Guidance Council)
Herbert Gray College
Little Church Street
Rugby
Warwickshire CV21 3AP
0788 573241

SPOD (Association to aid the Sexual and Personal Relationship of People with a Disability)
286 Camden Road
London N7 OBJ
071 607 8851

Smoking

More and more nowadays, people are tending to give up smoking — or rather, trying to give up smoking. There are many medical or herbal remedies available, but often counselling helps you to work through the emotions that may arise if withdrawal symptoms hit. One well-known method of dealing with smoking problems, and one which many people try as a first option is hypnosis or hypnotherapy. Hypnotherapists work with the subconscious mind to encourage you to give up. Most have high success rates in the short term, although we have had mixed reports of their long-term results since they are generally not equipped to deal with the emotions that can be thrown up as a result of stopping. Many counsellors will not accept you into counselling just for smoking cure, as they realize that smoking is simply a symptom of underlying issues, and insist that you are willing to work on these too before they will agree to counsel you. We frequently recommend people to go to a hynotherapist to give up, but then use a general counsellor to work through the emotions that come up, rather than wind up substituting another behaviour, such as eating, for smoking.

Suicide

Wanting to end your own life usually demands immediate emergency counselling. The best-known organization which has particular expertise in this area is the Samaritans. They offer a twenty-four hour telephone counselling service and also a befriending service to help you cope. You don't need to give your name, although they will probably ask you what it is, and they will respect your right to end your life if that is what you choose.

There may be other agencies in your area who offer telephone and face-to-face counselling. Also, if you feel this way often, you may want to seek regular counselling on the NHS. If you do attempt suicide and are admitted to hospital, you will be offered counselling there as soon as you feel well enough.

MIND
22 Harley Street
London W1 2ED
071 637 0741

Lifeline
148 Lonsdale Street
Melbourne
Victoria 3000
03 662 1677

Samaritans (Head Office)
17 Uxbridge Road
Slough SL1 1SN
0753 32713

Samaritans Australia
Consult your local area
phone directory.

Trauma

It has long been recognized that traumatic events, be they physical disasters or emotional crises, can create problems for us later. A single, very distressing event can lay the foundations for physical and mental symptoms in years to come. Crime victims and survivors of fire, flood or accident can suffer physical side-effects for which there is no obvious cause, as well as the more expected ones such as nightmares, anxiety, irritability and depression.

Up to now, counselling after trauma has usually been offered through the NHS, often after the sufferer has spent some time on tranquillizers. Private counsellors also offer long-term support, though we found few who specialized in this area. Recently, however, after the Zeebrugge and King's Cross disasters, the need for immediate trauma counselling has been recognized and special teams have been set up to help victims and relatives.

National Association of Victim Support Schemes
Cranmer House
39 Brixton Road
London SW9 5DZ
071 735 9166

Women's issues

There are a number of issues which have been largely covered elsewhere in this chapter but which can also be seen as women's issues; these include eating disorders, gynaecological problems, and rape and assault counselling. Whilst by no means excluding the possibility of men needing counselling on these, we wish to mention some women's centres which specialize in these issues.

Birmingham Women's Counselling and Therapy Centre
43 Ladywood Middleway
Birmingham B16 8HA
021 455 8677
(NHS-based self-referral service for long- and short-term individual and groupwork.)

London Women's Aid
52-54 Featherstone Street
London EC1 8RT
071 251 6537
(Support for victims of domestic violence.)

Women's Counselling and Therapy Service
Top floor
Oxford Chambers
Oxford Place
Leeds LS1 3AX
0532 455725
(Psychodynamic and humanistic counselling from a feminist perspective.)

Women's Health and Reproductive Rights Information Centre
52-54 Featherstone Street
London EC1Y 8RT
071 251 6580
(Gives general referral and information.)

Women's Therapy Centre
6 Manor Gardens
London N7 6LA
071 263 6200

Young people's counselling

Counselling for young people is a specialist field. If a child has problems or symptoms, then your first reaction may well be to take him or her for medical treatment, and your GP may then refer the child on for counselling within the NHS system. Alternatively, a young person may be receiving counselling or pastoral care at school for help with his or her education. We found only rare examples of young people being taken to private counsellors, and then usually for exam assistance or career guidance. The National Association of Young People's Counselling and Advisory Services coordinates those whose work is the counselling and advising of young people in the 16-25 age group and has contacts with 88 advisory agencies nationwide.

National Association for Gifted Children
Park Campus
Boughton Green Road
Northampton
NN2 7AL
0604 792300

NAYPCAS (National Association of Young People's Counselling and Advisory Service.)
The Magazine Business Centre
11 Newarke Street
Leicester LE1 5SS
0533 558763

Chapter 15

Consumer guide — schools

This book is a practical book, intended to show you the practical possibilities in counselling, and what you can gain from it. However, like all practical things, the activities we talk about are underpinned by ideas and theories. The session you have with your particular counsellor is, whether you are aware of it or not, set against a background of schools of counselling which are alive and well and living in Britain today.

The chapter contains:

- an outline of why there should be so many different and often conflicting schools of counselling
- a brief historical overview of how counselling has developed
- listings of the best established or most interesting of the schools.

Why different schools?

It may seem strange that in such a field as the development of increased human happiness, there is not more consensus. Surely we ought to be able to agree about what works and what doesn't?

The problem is this. Each school of psychology is based on some particular theory about how the mind works. Since the mind is so unbelievably complex, *all* of these theories are, in actual fact, gross oversimplifications; each theory reflects only those aspects of the mind that its inventor noticed or thought was important.

To make matters worse, it is virtually impossible to either prove or disprove any of these theories; you cannot take a mind apart to see how it works, like you can a car. The only real test of theories is whether they are actually useful to you, the client. And because this depends so much on the practitioner and the way *she* uses the theory, researchers find it very difficult to get consistent results.

So, in the absence of hard information, psychologists and counsellors, like priests and politicians, resort to dogma. Around each new theory arises a 'school' of people who are particularly impressed by either the theory or its originator, and, before you know it, they have an institute, a training school and all the other paraphenalia that goes with respectability. As we have stressed throughout the book, the best thing that you, the client, can do to navigate your own path through this jungle of schools and theories is to concentrate on the counsellor and how you get on with him or her. Only once you have established that the counsellor is the right *person* for you is it really worth your while to go into their theoretical background.

Historical overview

Psychology as a formal study began with the Ancient Greeks, but their vehicle for personal change was drama, rather than counselling. Aristotle wrote that,

> *Tragedy, then, is an imitation of an action of high importance. . . acted not narrated; by means of pity and fear effecting its purgation of these emotions.*[1]

The basic theory was 'purgation'; that you have some sort of emotional reservoir that must be emptied from time to time.

While the Greeks were the only ancient people to write

---

[1] Poetics (Duckworth 1987)

about psychology, they certainly weren't the only ones to use it. All over the pre-Christian world there was a rich Shamanistic tradition of folk psychology involving the use of drugs, symbols and trance. Although suppressed in Europe by the Christian churches, this never quite died out, and in the early 19th century one element of it, hypnosis, was revised and popularized by Mesmer. As a result of his work, hypnosis and hynotherapy still thrive, although possibly as a result of his outrageous showmanship and love of scandal, they have never attained the credibility they deserve.

It was almost a century later, in the early 1900s, that Sigmund Freud, with his rigorous scientific training as a neurologist, rejected the uncertainties of hypnosis in favour of analysis, in which the origins of psychological problems were discovered, and the original emotions purged (back to the Greeks again) by talking about them. Freud's dazzling array of theories led to the plethora of psychoanalytical and related schools that exist today. There is a negative side to his contribution, however, in that, by concentrating his attention on understanding how the mind works, he neglected the issue of how it might change. Had he not turned his back on hypnosis, but instead applied his genius to developing it, psychology might by now have become a tool for everyday enlightenment.

The next major developments in psychology matured in the 1950s, with two very different approaches. Carl Rogers invented the 'client-centred' approach. This developed and diversified to become humanistic psychology, which now embraces more schools and theories than the rest of psychology put together! Rogers, incidentally, was also the first to use the term 'counselling' in a psychotherapeutic context. And at around the same time, B.F. Skinner brought the behaviourist approach to fruition, with his idea that people could be 'conditioned' into being happy. His ideas have tended to be used more in schools and psychiatric hospitals. Individual behavioural counsellors have softened their approach into yet another 'talking' model.

Throughout the 1950s, Gregory Bateson and others were working on quite a different track. They were applying the mathematical models of systems theory to people, and looking in detail for the first time at the nature of people's interactions with each other. In the 1960s and '70s, their insights led to the development of systems psychology, encompassing several schools of family therapy as well as the more individually orientated transactional analysis and NLP.

So while there are hundreds of different schools of counselling, they all fall into one or more of these five broad categories; hypnotic, analytic, humanistic, behaviourist and systemic. If you can tease out which of these five categories your counsellor uses, you will at least have made a start in understanding why they do what they do. This summary is intended as a 'bird-spotter's manual' of counselling schools,[2] so if a counsellor comments that he is a humanist or a behaviourist, you will know what that says about his approach, and be able to judge him accordingly.

Remember, as always, however, that most counsellors mix and match approaches, and that in any case two counsellors trained in the same school will not neccessarily practise in the same way. Nevertheless, this chapter may help you make general assessments.

Please note that a listing in this chapter does not mean that we recommend, endorse or take responsibility for any organization or individual.

Schools

In most cases, the listings given here are *not* help-lines — the person who answers the phone will be able to give you information but not counsel you directly.

Behaviourism

Behaviourism starts with the notion that, since we don't know what is going on in the mind, we are better off concentrating on things we can observe directly; what goes in (what we see, hear, etc) and what comes out (what we do). When these two are obviously connected, this is known as

---

[2] For a more rigorous overview, try John Rowan and Windy Dryden's dyptych *Individual Therapy in Britain* and *Innovative Therapy in Britain* (see Bibliography).

stimulus and response; for example if a mother sees her baby smiling at her (stimulus), she may pick the baby up (response). Each time this happens, the baby's smiling is 'reinforced', and so, of course, the baby will develop the habit of smiling when it wants attention; this is known as conditioning. In the basic behaviourist model, any habitual behaviour is the result of conditioning, and the way to change that behaviour (assuming it is undesirable) is to reverse the conditioning by either reinforcing (rewarding) the opposite behaviour or by negatively reinforcing (penalizing) it.

In practice, this does not work very well, mainly because people resent being treated like that. So behaviour therapy has split into two streams. The early methods continue to be used in some hospitals; we have heard particular horror stories about the treatment of anorexics, amongst others. The second, much more sensitive stream, treats individual clients with more respect; behaviour therapists will work to help a client develop 'coping strategies' through various forms of mental training, or to change their own responses to certain stimuli, frequently by using fantasy to negatively reinforce old habits, and positively reinforce new ones. Until recently, behaviourist methods were widely regarded as the best way to deal with phobias.

British Association of Behavioural Psychotherapy
Mr Howard Lomas
c/o Social Services
7 Whittaker Street
Radcliffe
Manchester
M26 9TD
061 724 6321

Bioenergetics

Like that of many other counselling schools, bioenergetic theory says that our happiness stems from our very early experiences, including those in the womb. We can reach this 'material' only through certain forms of movement and breathing, but when we do reach and release it, we will start feeling good about ourselves.

If you are new to counselling, or have a very specific issue to work on this is probably not for you. It is very emotional and very noisy, and not very similar to anything you will have ever done before. If you have had counselling experience, however, and want long-term counselling that will tackle deep personality issues, bioenergetics can be both fun and releasing!

British Association for Bioenergetic Analysis
Open Centre
188 Old Street
London EC1
081 549 9583

British Institute of Bioenergetic Analysis (Bioenergetics Associates)
22 Fitzjohn's Avenue
London NW3
071 435 1079

Scottish Centre for Bioenergetic Analysis
c/o David Campbell
041 332 6371

Biodynamics

Developed through the work of Gerda Boyesen, Biodynamics is a regressive, cathartic school of counselling. The counsellor will spend a number of sessions massaging you and, in particular, listening to your stomach through a stethoscope to hear how its responses alter as the massage continues. As the sessions continue, you will also be encouraged to become more aware yourself of your body movements and allow them to develop into larger, more expressive signs of emotion. Your counsellor will encourage you to talk about what you are feeling and thinking.

Biodynamics would seem to be for you if you like to be touched and to talk through your issues only after a good deal of massage and body attention. This would be good for anyone who is aware that their problems are linked to the state of their body.

Gerda Boyesen Institute
Acacia House
Centre Avenue
Acton Park
London W3 7JX
081 743 2437

Brief counselling

A term used both to describe any counselling that takes a short time only, and any that is done to a client's requirements (a 'brief'). It can be used in conjunction with any kind of counselling.

Co-Counselling

Another predominantly regressive/cathartic form of counselling. The counselling is non-directive and supportive, and based very much on Rogerian ideas of listening and acceptance. The really interesting thing about Co-Counselling is its reciprocal nature; Co-Counsellors take it in turns to client and to counsel.

To Co-Counsel, you must first take a basic course. This takes at least forty hours, and is usually done in an evening or weekend group, sometimes residential. One-to-one teaching is also possible.

The advantages of Co-Counselling to us are its democracy, its emphasis on celebration, particularly the acceptance and celebration of emotional expression, and its low cost. Its dangers, as we have experienced them, are that Co-Counsellors can get so caught up in expressing negative emotion that they become 'discharge junkies' and fail to make the distinction between sessions and real life, feeling good only when they feel bad. Because of its self-directedness and peer structure, Co-Counselling is one of the 'ways in' to longer term involvement in personal development through the Growth movement.

Co-Counselling Phoenix
5 Victoria Road
Sheffield S10 2DJ
0742 686371

(Classes in and publication of literature on cathartic counselling including Co-Counselling. They produce a teacher's directory for Great Britain).

Encounter

Encounter groups are the original Growth movement activity. Under the direction of the group leader (or facilitator', a popular term throughout the Growth movement), participants interact, play games, do structured exercises and gradually become aware of how they are relating to each other. Great emphasis is put on saying what you really feel, however negative, rather than following social conventions of politeness. Issues between the group members are seen as significant, and are dealt with on the spot by direct confrontation of the feelings involved.

The Encounter model briefly is this: our idea of our self is formed largely by the way we relate to others. Often, because of our interactions, our self-image distorts. Only truthful, here-and-now, interactions between ourselves and other people can recreate our self-image in a relevant and helpful way.

Encounter groups are usually day, weekend or even weeklong, and are often residential. We would suggest that before joining a group, particularly if you have done very little counselling, you check with the group leader what is the level of risk and confrontation he is expecting in the group. Some encounter groups can offer incredibly supportive ways of learning how to relate; others are inhabited by people who enjoy confrontation for its own sake — if you can, find out about the group before you decide whether it is for you.

Open Centre
188 Old Street
London EC1
081 549 9583

EST

See *The Forum*.

Existential counselling

Very much a cerebral form of counselling, existential counselling is based on the idea that you only arrive at true development via the long hard route of examining yourself and how you see the world.

Sessions will normally extend over a long time, and are typified by both client and counsellor attempting to be super-honest in how they see themselves, each other and the world. There is a lot of checking out, a lot of interpretation, explanation, definition of what is going on. The client-counsellor relationship is analysed too. Although existential counselling has been described as relevant to the total person, we would not expect to find a great deal of body-work going on in a session. Definitely only an option for people with plenty of time and money. To find out more contact:

Philadelphia Association
4 Marty's Yard
17 Hampstead High Street
London NW3 1PX
071 794 2652 (Afternoons, Ansaphone otherwise)

Emmy van Deurzen-Smith, Dean
Society for Existential Analysis
School of Psychotherapy and Counselling
Regent's College
Inner Circle, Regent's Park
London NW1
071 487 7556

Family therapy

Family therapists point out that counselling one person is often not sufficient. One person's symptom can often be an expression of a problem belonging to a whole family, and if that person starts to change, the family dynamic will drag them back. Effecting a permanent change might well be a matter of ignoring the person with the symptom altogether, and working exclusively with other members of the family. So, for example, if a teenager was depressed or violent, a family therapist would counsel her parents, brothers and sisters too. The sessions might involve one-to-one work, or group discussion. One member of the family might be 'tasked' to behave in a certain way towards the others, in order to change a group dynamic which was leading to the problem behaviour in the first place. Many other approaches can be used under the general framework of Family Therapy.

Institute of Family Therapy
43 New Cavendish Street
London W1M 7RG
071 935 1651

Feminist counselling

Feminist counselling is not so much a specific school as an approach to counselling as a whole. Feminist counsellors can be analytical or humanistic; what binds them together is their social and political perspective. They believe in equal relationships between people without the hierarchical structure that society (and many therapies) has, with the power given to men and to male values. So, for example, feminist therapists will be very careful that the client, be they male or female, is fully involved in the decision-making process of sessions.

Birmingham Women's Counselling and Therapy Centre
43 Ladywood Middleway
Birmingham B16 8HA
021 455 8677
(NHS self-referral service for individual and group work.)

Women's Counselling and Therapy Service
Oxford Chambers
Oxford Place
Leeds LS1 3AX
0532 455725
(Psychodynamic and humanistic counselling from a feminist perspective.)

Women's Therapy Centre
6 Manor Gardens
London N7 6LA
071 263 6200

The Forum

Re-named and re-vamped version of the famous EST training, The Forum uses behavioural principles to create an
intense experience intended to change your whole approach
to life to a more positive and goal-orientated one. We include
The Forum as representative of a genre of intense (and
intensely controversial) training which, to some degree,
models the experience of religious conversion. People who
stick with it think it is the answer to everything; people who
reject it condemn it as, at best, manipulative and, at worst,
evil. We think counselling falling into this school would be
most useful to people who have already developed a strong
sense of self-esteem. If you are still desperately searching
for 'the answer', however, we would advise that you choose
something that is more clearly psychotherapeutic.

Gestalt

Developed by Fritz Perls, Gestalt counselling holds that, as
everything that happens to us happens in the present, it
is the present that we should be exploring in counselling.
Although Gestalt, like many other essentially humanistic
disciplines, accepts that past, particularly early childhood
events, formed the basis of our personalities, the emphasis
in counselling is on looking at thoughts, feelings and
behaviours as they occur, stepping free of 'shoulds' and
'woulds' and exploring what is real for us here and now.

Gestalt counselling can take place in group workshops or
in one-to-one sessions. In order to contact the here and now,
a counsellor might suggest that a client raises awareness of
her feelings by repeating certain gestures or words, or by
exaggerating slight movements to focus attention on them.
Gestalt is best known for using role play, putting significant
characters in a client's life on a cushion or in a chair and
talking to them as if they were there, or doing the same with
parts of their mind, treated as if they are separate individuals.

Many counsellors who espouse other methods also use
Gestalt techniques; they underpin a great deal of the humanistic counselling used today.

The Gestalt Centre
64 Warwick Road
St Alban's
Herts AL1 4DL
0727 864806

Lifespace
100 Gloucester Road
London SW7 4AU
071 584 8819

Open Centre
188 Old Street
London EC1
081 549 9583

Humanistic approach

A generic term to indicate that the counsellor has a particular approach to counselling. In general, a humanistic counsellor will be offering a client-centred approach, probably with lots of touch and body awareness, almost certainly with the emphasis on positive goal setting and a supportive relationship between client and counsellor.

Hypnotherapy

Hypnotherapy nowadays is sometimes seen as an 'easy option', a way to short-circuit the perceived struggle of long-term counselling. It is therefore often seen as a method of 'fixing' symptoms such as smoking or weight-gain. It is also unfortunate that many hypnotherapy training courses are so short that they and their participants have gained a bad reputation. We feel that both these factors have meant a devaluation of hypnotherapy, which is a real tool capable of creating real change.

A good hypnotherapist will take the time to find out what your goals are, and check that what you want is compatible with your life-style and to the good of youself and people around you, otherwise your unconscious is very unlikely to co-operate. She will suggest that you relax and allow your mind to become calm. It is likely that, contrary to the many hypnotism clichés, she won't use a bright object to catch your attention, but will simply encourage you to get comfortable in your chair. Then she will speak to your unconscious mind directly, asking for its help in achieving your outcome. You will probably *not* forget all that has happened. In any case, whether you do or not is no indication of the effectiveness of the counselling!

Good hypnotherapy can do deep and effective work. However as with all schools we mention, you need to be sure that you are working with a trained and ethical practitioner. It won't provide you with a chance to talk or get emotional with your counsellor. If you want insight or support, it may not be the most appropriate method for you.

National Register of Hypnotherapists and Psychotherapists
12 Cross Street
Nelson
Lancashire
BB9 7EN
0282 699378

Society for Primary Cause Analysis by Hypnosis
13 Beechwood Rd
Sanderstead
South Croydon
CR2 0AE
081 657 3624

Neuro-Linguistic Programming

The most recent (and in our view, the finest) expression of the systemic approach, NLP is concerned with achieving the most profound and most appropriate personal change in the shortest possible time. Until recently, NLP had no therapeutic techniques that it could fairly call its own; instead, like Japan's post-war technologists, it pirated methods from other schools and fine-tuned them through the application of systemic and linguistic theory. As with the Japanese, the result was something that was more reliable and took less time and energy on the part of both client and counsellor.

Since 1985, NLP practitioners have had at their disposal both versions of just about everyone else's techniques, and a technique unique to NLP: changing feelings directly through altering the form (size, brightness and so on) of mental images. Done properly, this can change lifelong problems in the space of a few minutes. (Done badly, of course, they have the same result as any bad work; the client gets annoyed and goes off to find a better counsellor.)

NLP is for you if you are either in a hurry to make a specific personal change, or if you have a 'generative' goal such as 'to be happy' or 'to boost my career'. You will probably not find NLP useful if you need a good deal of long-term support or deep catharsis. One warning though: the power of the techniques has led some practitioners to think that they can become professional counsellors before they are, in fact, ready. As with all counsellors, follow the golden rule of trusting a personal recommendation and gut responses above all else.

Association for Neuro-Linguistic Programming
100b Carysfort Road
London N16 9AP
071 241 3664 (Also a fax number)

Person-centred counselling

Based on the work of Carl Rogers, person-centred counselling contradicts the idea that the counsellor is the expert and the client is there to follow suggestions and listen to advice. Rogers' work was revolutionary in the middle years of this century, and has now become the basis of most humanistic methods. He believed that if the counsellor was open, responsive and approving, the client would contact her own personal resources and inner strength.

Most humanistic disciplines would therefore be using Rogers' methods of listening in an empathetic manner, asking open-ended questions and validating the client's point of view. Because it is a gentle and supportive approach, such counselling seems particularly suitable for beginners.

Personal Construct Theory

Enormously complex in theory, PCT is based on the idea that we see the world through 'constructs', mental spectacles that colour our perception. We can't take these spectacles off, but we can change their lenses to ones that are more useful to us. The therapist's job is to work out what sort of constructs you have that are causing distress, and to find a way to change them. The favoured tools are writing, talking and role-play; you might be asked to write about yourself as you are or how you want to be, you will certainly be asked a great many questions and you may find yourself agreeing to play different roles either in the session itself or in the weeks between. The format varies widely since George Kelly, PCT's founder, insisted that any change technique could be validly used within the theoretical framework that he had set out. The examples we have come across were relatively short-term with sessions once a week, so probably worth a try if quick(ish) change is what you are after.

Centre for Personal Construct Psychology
132 Warwick Way
London SW1V 4JD
071 834 8875

Play therapy

We use the term here to mean firstly any counselling which utilizes toys or play methods — for example, where children are asked to act out a distressing scene at home by using dolls to signify parents. Secondly, and to us more interestingly, play therapy can be a chance for adults to play, a chance they are not often given in life. Real opportunity to play, in a one-to-one session or in a workshop, can result not only in regressive work but also in increased feelings of freedom, openness and creativity. Everyone should have some play therapy at some time in their lives!

Primal Integration

This is another counselling school which lays the emphasis on very early times in our lives, even going back to conception. When our early needs are not met, we suffer but we are powerless to do anything about it. This leads us to feel bad about ourselves and unable to fulfil our potential. The idea is that in counselling, when we get in touch with this very early pain and express the hurt of it, we gain insight and, if this is integrated into our adult lives, we can begin to fulfil ourselves again, emotionally, mentally and even spiritually.

Primal sessions are based around heavy catharsis, which is encouraged by the counsellor using breathing and other techniques to take the client right back to very early memories. Sometimes, in an attempt to recreate the birth experience, a counsellor will bury the client in cushions or put weight on her — this is most often done in group sessions where all the group members can lend their support.

Primal Integration can be done one-to-one or in workshop groups of varying lengths and intensities. As with all deeply cathartic schools, this is appropriate for you if you feel the need to experience deep and powerful emotion, not so suitable if you want a gentle or intellectual approach.

International Primal Association
c/o 79 Pembroke Road
London E17 9BB
081 521 4764

London Association of Primal Psychotherapists
18a Laurier Road
London NW5 1SH
071 267 9616 (Office hours Tuesday, Wednesday; Friday 12-1pm; Thursday 11-12)
(Patients for trainee therapists taken at a lower rate.)

Open Centre
188 Old Street
London EC1
081 549 9583

Provocative therapy

Based on systems theory and invented in the USA by Frank Farrelly; we were unable to track down any of his followers in the UK. Working with an individual or a family, the counsellor is as provocative as possible in order to flick the client's mind over some threshold into a world of new possibilities. There are many wonderful stories about the essence of Provocative Therapy, which illustrate just how wild, unpredictable behaviour on the part of a counsellor can jolt a client out of unhappiness, their mental loops or even their clinical schizophrenia and help them begin to relate happily in the world.

Psychoanalysis/psychodynamic counselling

Psychoanalytic theory holds that the prime aim of psychoanalysis is to unblock the unconscious from its conflicts by encouraging self-exploration which begins with the counsellor and ends with the client in a continuous process of self-analysis.

Freud invented psychoanalysis; parallel schools were subsequently founded by Jung, who was concerned with myth and symbol; Klein who was concerned with the early months as a formative period in life; and Adler, who was concerned more with the future and with inner dialogue. All these schools will typically ask you to commit for up to five sessions a week for possibly two years, and we have heard of ten- or twelve-year commitments.

Nowadays, some of the stereotypes of psychoanalysis are outdated. Many counsellors no longer use a couch, and most no longer try to convince their clients that everything is sexually based. However, psychoanalysis is still often a long-term and expensive form of counselling; it won't suit you if you want warm support with lots of touching, if you prefer a great deal of cathartic emotion, if you like a non-interpretive approach or if you are after measurable results.

Adlerian Society of Great Britain
161 Charlton Church Lane
081 858 1767/7299

Association of Jungian Analysts
Flat 3
7 Eton Avenue
London NW3 3EL
071-794 8711

Group Analytic Practice
88 Montagu Mansions
London W1H 1LF
071 935 3103

Institute of Psychotherapy and Social Studies
18 Laurier Road
London NW5 15G
071 284 4762

Isis Centre
43 Little Clarendon Street
Oxford
OX1 2HS
0865 56648
(Self-referral counselling service.)

C G Jung Clinic (Society for Analytical Psychology)
1 Daleham Gardens
London NW3 5BY
071 435 7696

NAFSIYAT
The Intercultural Therapy Centre
278 Seven Sisters Road
London N4 2HY
071 263 4130
(Psychotherapy for ethnic minorities.)

Scottish Institute of Human Relations
56 Albany Street
Edinburgh EH1 3QR
031 556 0924

Tavistock Clinic
120 Belsize Lane
London NW3 5BA
071 435 7111

Westminster Pastoral Foundation
23 Kensington Square
London W8 5HN
071 937 6956

Psychodrama

Mentioned also in Chapter 14 as a technique that can be used in a group session or workshop, psychodrama is a school of its own. By 'acting out' issues, or the memories that underpin them, we can gain understanding, insight, and often emotional release.

Psychodrama can take many forms, though it is usually done in groups. Long-term workshops of a weekend or a week are probably the best, because then most people in the group have the chance to be the focus of attention, and role-play their issues with the group. You can play yourself, get someone else to play you, play another person in your particular scenario, or all three! Whatever you choose, directing the acting out of some crucial event in your life, past or future, can be both fascinating and enlightening; if some particular break-through is achieved, or if you feel in need, the group is there to support you. After this, you can talk about what you have learned, and even practise how the 'new you' will behave in the future.

We would recommend Psychodrama if done in a well-run group, particularly as when your turn comes, you can take very direct control, choosing just how far you want to be involved.

Gale Centre
Whitakers Way
Loughton
Essex IG10 1SQ
081 508 9344

Holwell Centre for Psychodrama and Sociodrama
East Down
Barnstaple
Devon EX31 4NZ
0271 50597/850267
(Residential centre.)

Morpeth Centre for Psychotherapy
40 Grosvenor Place
Jesmond
Newcastle-on-Tyne
NE2 2RE
091 281 6243

Open Centre
188 Old Street
London EC1
081 549 9583

Psychosynthesis

Psychosynthesis draws on a great many techniques from a variety of sources. Writing, drawing, symbolism, imaging, dreamwork and subpersonalities are called upon to shed light on what has happened in our past and how it is contributing to our present problem. There is a great deal of awareness paid to what is going on inside our minds and bodies as well as outside, and to developing this faculty of awareness.

Psychosynthesis seems to us a respectful and gentle counselling technique suitable for those entering counselling for the first time, as well as those who wish to make a longer-term commitment. You need to be able to accept a certain spiritual (as opposed to religious) orientation, and it is certainly not for those who want specific problems to be 'fixed' quickly.

Institute of Psychosynthesis
The Barn
Nan Clark's Lane
Mill Hill
London NW7 4HH
081 959 2330

Psychosynthesis and Education Trust
48-50 Guildford Road
Stockwell SW8 2BN
071 622 8295

Rational-emotive therapy

Based on the theory that we are in search of happiness although we defeat ourselves in this quest constantly by buying into irrational personal philosophies. The aim of the rational-emotive therapist is to help clients achieve this happiness by helping them set goals, and then use instruction, direction and tasks to help achieve them.

The session style tends to be directive; counsellors ask direct questions and challenge clients' statements. They can use behavioural techniques (qv) such as reward and penalization (see chapter 5) and often set tasks to keep clients on track. The idea is to enable clients to see that it is only their own irrationality that keeps them from getting to where they want to go.

If you are very goal-orientated and think you can change your beliefs by talking about them in a fairly intellectual way, then rational-emotive therapy may be for you.

Rational-emotive therapy
c/o 14 Winchester Avenue
London NW6 7TU
071 624 0732

Transactional Analysis

Based on a stunningly simple model of human interaction (we will die happy if we develop anything remotely as aesthetically pleasing...) Eric Berne's school of Transactional Analysis has to be the least pretentious thing ever to come out of psychology. Simply put, it suggests that each of us has three subpersonalities — the Parent, the Adult and the Child. The Parent part of us is the one which internally criticizes, but can also support and nourish us; the Child is that part of us which can be delightfully spontaneous, but also childishly disobedient or insolent. The Adult is wise, realistic and centred. We can analyse what is happening inside us in terms of how the parts of us interact. We can also analyse what is happening between us and other people (i.e. transactions) when, for example, our Child meets someone else's Child and we both end up helpless with giggles; or when our Child meets someone else's Parent — we wind them up and they get more and more critical.

The ultimate goal of Transactional Analysis is for all parts of us to respond to others on an equally respectful level: 'I'm OK, you're OK'. But if we disapprove of others by elevating ourselves (I'm OK, you're not OK) or put ourselves down by elevating others (You're OK, I'm not OK) then there is distress.

TA groups or one-to-one counselling teach this model and then use it to analyse what is happening within us and between us and others. Counsellors or group leaders can vary in style from very warm and creative to very challenging and confrontative. The real progress happens when you take the model on board and start using it to gain insights about what is happening for you and change that.

Institute for Transactional Analysis
BM Box 4104
London
WC1N 3XX
071 404 5011

Lifespace
100 Gloucester Road
London SW7 4AU
071 584 8819

Open Centre
188 Old Street
London EC1
081 549 9583

Transpersonal Psychology

Another more spiritually based counselling school, which concentrates on 'self-realization'. Along with many other schools, the Transpersonal Psychology belief is that unhappy early experiences lead us to adopt certain ways of behaving that protect us, but which, later in life, become inappropriate if we want to fulfil our potential.

The Transpersonal school has a limited number of counsellors in Britain, though more are being trained each year. They run a full programme of workshops. Their ways of working include imagery, dreams, daydreams, meditation, writing, drawing, painting, 'putting people on chairs' as in Gestalt. A typical session might involve a guided fantasy offering lots of opportunity to imagine various scenarios linked with your issue, and then some time looking at what images and symbols you contacted within your guided fantasy.

We feel that if you enjoy working with such techniques and would welcome self-development with a slightly spiritual approach, then Transpersonal Psychology would be suitable for you.

Centre for Transpersonal Psychology
7 Pembridge Place
London W2 4XB
(All enquiries in writing please.)

General contracts

These organizations can either offer you more than one form of counselling, or can refer you to particular practitioners in the fields you want. Most of these do not offer emergency counselling. If you need this, ring the Samaritans or one of the other help-lines listed earlier in the book.

Tom Allan Centre
23 Elm Bank Street
Glasgow G2 4PB
041 221 1535
(Pastoral counselling service offering one-to-one, marital and group therapy.)

Alton Counselling Service
Friends Meeting House
Church House
Alton
Hampshire
0420 89207

Blackpool and Fylde Counselling Centre
Beaufort Avenue
Bispham
Blackpool
0253 56624/867197

British Association for Counselling
37a Sheep Street
Rugby
Warwickshire
CV21 3BX
0788 578328/9
(Referrals throughout Great Britain.)

Carrs Lane Counselling Centre
Carrs Lane Centre
Birmingham
B4 7SX
021 643 6363

Centre for Counselling and Psychotherapy Education
21 Lancaster Road
London W11 1QL
071 221 3215
(Marriage/family/individual counselling.)

Chelsea Pastoral Foundation (counselling for young people)
155a Kings Road
Chelsea
London SW3 5TX
071 351 0839

Independent Counselling and Advisory Service
PO Box 615
Aspley Guise
Milton Keynes
MK17 8DB
0908 281128
(Counselling services to organizations.)

Institute of Psychotherapy and Social Studies
18 Laurier Road
London NW5 1SG
071 284 4762
(Analytic and humanistic counselling.)

Karuna Core Therapies
Karuna Institute
Foxhole
Dartington
Totnes
Devon TQ9 6EB
0803 867940

Minster Centre
57 Minster Road
London NW2 3SH
071 435 9200
(A training organization which offers low-cost counselling.)

Monkton Wyld Court
Nr. Charmouth
Bridport
Dorset DT6 6DQ
0297 60342

Morpeth Centre for Psychotherapy
40 Grosvenor Place
Jesmond
Newcastle-on-Tyne
NE2 2RE
091 281 6243

Norwich Centre for Personal and Professional Development
7 Earlham Road
Norwich NR2 3RA
0603 617709

Open Centre
188 Old Street
London EC1
071 549 9583

South London Growth Centre
66 Brixton Water Lane
London SW2
071 274 6531

Wrekin Trust
Runnings Park
Croft Bank
West Malvern
Worcs WR14 4BP
0684 892898

Also try your local GP, Health Centre, or Community Health Council.

Training organizations

The following offer general courses in counselling, or can refer you on to relevant courses in the field that interests you.

Centre for Counselling and Psychotherapy Education
21 Lancaster Road
London W11 1QL
071 221 3215

The Facilitator Development Institute
The Norwich Centre
7 Earlham Road
Norwich NR2 3RA
0603 617709 (Manned 1-3pm)

Human Potential Resource Group
Dept of Adult Education
University of Surrey
Guildford GU2 5HX
0483 509191

Institute of Psychotherapy and Social Studies
18 Laurier Road
London NW5 1SG
071 284 4762

Metanola Psychotherapy Training Institute
13 North Common Road
London W5
081 579 2505

The Minster Training Centre
57 Minster Road
London NW2 3SH
071 435 9200

Morpeth Centre for Psychotherapy
40 Grosvenor Place
Jesmond
Newcastle-on-Tyne
NE2 2RE
091 281 6243

Outreach Counselling Courses
The Sternberg Centre
The Manor House
80 East End Road
London N3 2SY
081 346 2288

Richmond Fellowship
8 Addison Road
Kensington
London W14 8DL
071 603 6373/4/5

Westminster Pastoral Foundation
23 Kensington Square
London W8 5HN
071 937 6956

Bibliography

This is a very personal bibliography which includes books we have found particularly useful both in our own personal work, our counselling and in writing this book. We therefore do not list reference books for every issue or approach we mention; if you want to read further around any of them, however, the organizations we have listed will usually be happy to refer you to their magazines or a relevant 'starter' book in the field.

Co-Counselling

How to Change Yourself and Your World, Evison R. and Horobin R.W., Co-counselling Phoenix, (Sheffield, 1985).
For those who have done the basic course, but interesting for theory.

Family Therapy

Foundations of Family Therapy, Hoffman L., Basic Books, (New York, 1981).
Heavyweight introduction to the systemic schools of family therapy.

Feminist

In our Own Hands, Ernst S. and Goodison L., The Women's Press, (London, 1981).
Feminist self-help therapy. Excellent coverage of group work.

Gay

The Lavender Couch, Hall, Dr M., Alyson Publications (Boston, Massachusetts, 1985).
How to choose a counsellor, specifically aimed at lesbians and gay men.

General

Individual Therapy in Britain, Ed. Windy Dryden, Harper and Row (London, 1984).
Covers more traditional therapies, from psychoanalytic/psychodynamic onwards.

Innovative Therapy in Britain, Ed. Windy Dryden and John Rowan, Open University Press (Milton Keynes, 1988).
Covers the 'newer' therapies up to and including NLP.

Humanistic

The Reality Game, Rowan, J., Routledge & Kegan Paul, (London, 1983).
Overview aimed at 'people who are, or want to be, counsellors or psychotherapists'.

Hypnotherapy

Uncommon Therapy, Haley, J., McLeod, (Toronto, 1973).
Anecdotes and explanations of the work of Milton H. Erickson, widely regarded as the greatest exponent of the art and also massively influential in several other schools.

Negotiation

Getting to Yes, Fisher W. and Ury R., MIT Press, Boston, Massachusetts 1981.

NLP

Magic Demystified, Lewis, B.A., and F. Pucelik, Metamorphous Press (Oregon, 1982)
Simple text-book explanations

Using Your Brain — For A Change, Bandler, R., Real People Press (Moab UT, 1985)
Exciting and empowering — NLP changes in your own life

Peer group work

Co-operative and Community Group Dynamics, Randall, R. and J. Southgate, Barefoot Books, (London, 1980)
Pamphlet-style gem extolling, amongst other things, Will-helm Reich's Creative Orgasmic Theory of group process.

Primal integration/bioenergetics

Secret Life of the Unborn Child, Verny, T., Sphere (London, 1982).

Psychosynthesis

What We May Be, Ferrucci, P., Thorsons (Wellingborough, 1982).
Exercises and things to do plus interesting basic ideas

Transactional analysis

Games People Play, Berne, E., Penguin (Harmondsworth 1964)
The basic TA textbook

Other books of interest

Uncommon therapy, Haley, J., W.W. Norton and Co. (1973).
Steps to an Ecology of Mind, Bateson, G., Ballantine Books (1972)

Where to get them

Some of these books are popular enough to be tracked down relatively easily, others may strain the resources of your local bookshop. We have found two bookshops that will not only reliably come up with the goods, but will also send you books in the post.

Changes
242 Belsize Road
London NW6
01 328 5161

Compendium
234 Camden High Street
London
NW1
01 485 8944

Index